Foreword

Heysham Heritage Association is very pleased to b Heysham as a companion volume to *The Heysham Pen.* ....um Festival Awards for All programme.

The *Heysham Peninsula* is a compilation of contributions from many Association members and others, and focuses largely on more recent history. By contrast *The History of Heysham* is a personal contribution by one member of the Association and contains much greater detail of older history, setting Heysham into the wider context of the history of the British Isles. The Association congratulates the author on all the research and effort that has gone into compiling a fascinating account. Even when working from the same primary and other sources historians frequently come to different conclusions; conscious of this he has consulted others in the Association to clarify detail on several matters to ensure that all the interpretations recorded here are supported by reliable and accountable historical sources.

The history of Britain is traced from the times of the Celts, through the Roman occupation and the invasions by Angles, Saxons, Danes and Norsemen, and finally the Norman conquest. Then through the Middle Ages to the Reformation and Civil War; finally through the industrial revolution to the building of the Harbour and then modern times. St Patrick's Chapel is identified as an early focal point in both Celtic and Roman Christianity and later the Manor of Heysham plays a key role. Important national religious, royal and political personalities are identified, linking Heysham into the wider vision of history; and at the local level family histories are seen to play a significant role.

In conclusion the author sees Heysham emerging into a new era. No doubt he has partly in mind the recent acquisition by the National Trust of some of the coastal land, and the restoration by the Heritage Trust for the North West of a listed building in Main Street for use as a Heritage Centre, now run locally by our Association. The interest shown by these bodies is a witness to why Heysham has such an important role in the history of our region and country.

We have found this book a very good read and feel sure that others will find it likewise.

John Holding

Heysham Heritage Association

This book and its companion volume, *The Heysham Peninsula,* in the Millennium Festival series, have been printed by

The Charlesworth Group, Huddersfield.

Supported by
Millennium Awards for All

The History of Heysham by © David Flaxington
Published by Heysham Heritage Association (HHA)
Secretary: Barbara Verhoef, 80 Twemlow Parade, Heysham LA3 2AL
The Author has kindly granted HHA permission to publish a
limited edition (2000 copies) of The History of Heysham.
All proceeds from the sale of this book will go to HHA funds for conservation of
the heritage of Heysham, in particular the Heritage Centre.
The copyright of the text remains with the author.
The copyright of the images remains with the originators.

HHA was founded in 1990 and has over 100 members.
It is a voluntary society devoted to the heritage of Heysham.

HHA works in partnership with
the Heritage Trust for the North West, Registered Charity No. 508300

ISBN 0 9530303 4 2

The History of Heysham

A wide-angled view

by

David Flaxington

History, with its flickering lamps
stumbles along the trail of the past,
trying to reconstruct its themes,
to revive its echoes
and kindle with pale gleams
the passion of former days.
(Winston S Churchill : 1874 - 1965)

Heritage
H
E
Y
S
H Mesolithic Scraper
Association
M

2001

Bibliography & Acknowledgements

As most researchers are aware no complete list of sources can be given. Notes are gathered over a long period of time from libraries and countless other sources both public and private until the task of correlating them begins.

Significant sources referred to during the compilation of this manuscript were:

Trevor James (Ed.) : *Everyman's Encyclopedia* : Orbit
T Pape : *Heysham Old Hall* : Mitchell's Breweries
The Burke's Peerage : World Books
The First Book of Kings and Queens : Paragon Books
Baines : *History, Directory and Gazetteer of the County Palatine of Lancaster* (1825)
Farrer & Brownhill (eds) : *Victoria History of the Counties of England, Vol 8* :
    University of London, Institute of Historical Research (1914, rev. 1966)
Emmeline Garnett : *John Marsden's Will* : Hambledon & London Ltd (1998)
The Bayeux Tapestries
Thomas Hinde (ed.) : *The Domesday Book* : Coombe Books
James Taylor (ed.) : *The Family History of England*
Marion Yass : *The English Aristocracy* : Wayland
John Rhys : *Celtic Britain* : Senet Publications
British Kings and Queens : Brockhampton Press
Heysham Rectory Auxiliary Hospital Gazette (1917)
The Heysham Parish Magazine (various)

Special thanks to John Holding who did the typesetting and image processing (using Impression Publisher and Imagemaster on a RiscPC), and also for all the additional information, illustrations (pp.vi, 34, 53), suggestions and constructive criticism which he has provided.

Particular thanks to Robert Hargreaves (Wilson Grove, Heysham) for the cover design and images, and also for the image on p.28.

Thanks also are due to:

Beatrice Tollitt (Bailey Lane, Heysham : image p. 52 and text pp.66-67)
Andrew White & Nigel Dalziel (Lancaster City and Maritime Museums: image p.62)
Leslie Morgan (Heysham: for the Roy Woodhouse etching, p.46)
Tony Ross (West End, Morecambe: image(coin) p.1)
William Mitchell Barker (Mitchells of Lancaster Ltd)
Mike Whalley (retired Editor of The Visitor, Morecambe)
Bob Crabtree (Barrows Lane, Heysham)
John L Parkinson (Port Superintendent, Heysham Harbour (retired))
Malcolm and Carl Haynes (Heysham)
Norman Gibson (Twemlow Parade, Heysham)
Jim Wyatt (St Patrick's Walk, Heysham)
Other images: British Museum (p.59), Rheged Centre (p.25), The Visitor (p.70)

And last, but not least, thanks to Ann, my wife, for her unceasing activities on my behalf.

The History of Heysham
Contents

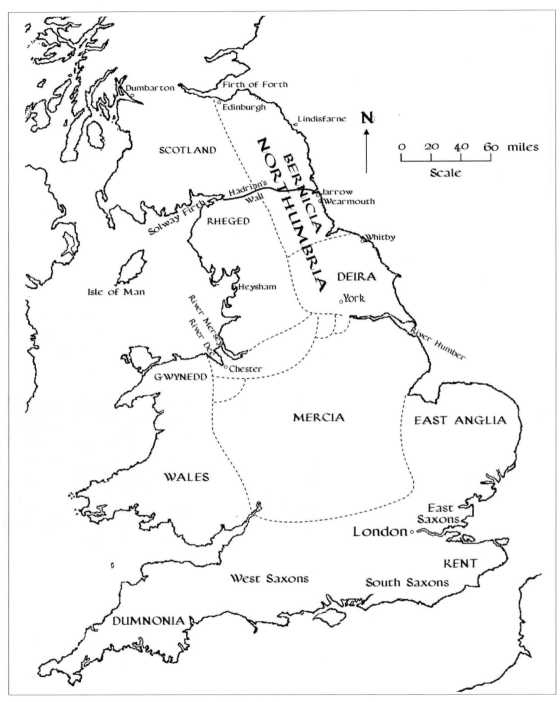

Dumbarton

Firth of Forth

Edinburgh

Lindisfarne

N

SCOTLAND

BERNICIA

NORTHUMBRIA

0   20   40   60 miles

Scale

Hadrian's Wall

Jarrow
Wearmouth

Solway Firth

RHEGED

Whitby

Isle of Man

Heysham

DEIRA

York

River Mersey

River Humber

River Dee

Chester

GWYNEDD

MERCIA

EAST ANGLIA

WALES

East
Saxons

London

KENT

West Saxons

South Saxons

DUMNONIA

Anglo-Saxon and Celtic Kingdoms
c. 450 - 700 AD

1. In the beginning ...

In the beginning there was land, and the Lord saw the land, and the land was good, and it came to be called

Heysham.

About 10,000 BC, when Heysham's earliest inhabitants made their home at the foot of the cliff on which St Patrick's Chapel now stands, Heysham must have been the most habitable area for many miles around.

With the ice-cover inching its way northwards over the centuries, inhospitable open marshland covered most low-lying areas, while at Heysham there were over 500 acres of firmer ground situated well above a sea-level much lower then than it is today. The little tribe of hunter-gatherers who made their home not far from the water's edge had stumbled upon the area's prime site.

Protected at the time by surrounding rocks, with fish in the sea and reindeer and elk roaming the area, little wonder their descendants made Heysham their home (albeit intermittently) for another 6,000 years, according to archaeologists from Lancaster University.

At the time, although Britain was still attached to mainland Europe, the population of England is believed to have numbered no more than a few thousand. Later, with the gradual melting of the remaining glaciers, the seas swelled to an unprecedented level and Britain became an island.

After a further 6000 years of erosion, agricultural disturbance and later development, all trace of Heysham's ancient history has been lost until around 80 AD, over three decades after the Romans first arrived in Britain.

Until recently there was no evidence of Roman presence at Heysham (apart from a coin found while excavating Heysham Harbour), but over the years amateur archaeologists have scoured Heysham's new development sites and uncovered a substantial number of Roman coins. A

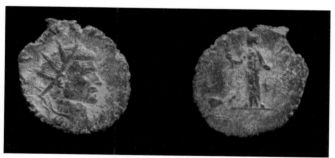

Roman Bronze Coin
Claudius II 268-270 AD

Roman dock further along the coast about a mile north of Carnforth testifies to their presence along the entire coastal area. Letters sent to the south of England by a Roman military commander in 81 AD are said to mention a tribe in the Morecambe/ Heysham area called the Setantii, of a people known collectively as 'Brigantes', who painted themselves blue with woad and continually attacked the Roman encampment.

An early tribal map of Britain names most of northern England 'Brigantes', with the coastal area between the Mersey and the Kent estuary named 'Setantii'. These 'blue-painted savages' worshipped the sun, the letters state, and Druids were their priests.

Throughout the centuries people of different races from many parts of the world had made their way to Britain. Most were from Europe and the Mediterranean, while others came from as far away as Assyria and beyond. Some later Druidic practices, although much diffused, appear to reflect certain practices common to the Sumerian priesthood of ancient Mesopotamia, the birthplace of civilization.

New burial practices were introduced, and monoliths and stone circles began to appear, the greatest of these being the awesome Stonehenge which took over 1000 years to complete. Now claimed by modern-day 'Druids' this gigantic example of ancient engineering was built in stages by successive generations of immigrants, including the mysterious 'Beaker People'.

Britain's Celts (a combination of race and culture) came originally from central and western Europe where they were the predominant element long before the rise of Rome. Various tribes began their spasmodic migration to Britain around 700 BC to find a land already inhabited by an agricultural, peasant population who lived mostly on farms, reared live-stock for food, used ox-drawn ploughs and bronze implements, and were already trading with Europe.

Although blue-painted and fearsome when in battle the Celts were far from being savages, despite the loathsome rituals of their adopted Druidic priesthood. Having inherited and in some cases improved upon their predecessor's agricultural techniques, Celtic tribes lived mostly in villages in mud-coated wickerwork houses. They wore a sleeved blouse and trousers fitting close to the ankle, with a tartan plaid across the shoulder fastened by a brooch, like the highlanders of later years who were their descendants.

Hilltop forts housed the more prosperous villages until a later incoming Celtic tribe from Northern Gaul destroyed the forts and built their own houses on the sites. Shortly afterwards came the Romans who occupied Britain for three-and-a-half centuries.

After facing spasmodic but fierce resistance for several decades a succession of Roman military leaders from the time of Julius Caesar onwards gradually conquered the British tribes south of what is now the Scottish border, and most resistance ended. Togodumus, high king of all the tribes, died in the fighting during a two day battle at the river Medway in 43 AD; his brother Caradoc (Caractacus), king of the Catavellauni tribe, escaped and fought on fiercely for another six years before being captured and taken to Rome; and Boudicca (Boadicea), Queen of the Iceni, is believed to have committed suicide in 60 AD after her savage but just rebellion was finally crushed. Only the Pictish-Scottish tribes of the north remained free of Roman domination.

According to the Roman chronicler Tacitus, the Druids

> deemed it a duty to their deities to cover their altars with the blood of captives, and to seek the will of the gods in the entrails of men.

When accompanying the Celts into battle these fearsome priests,

> pouring forth dire imprecations, with hands uplifted towards the heavens, struck terror into the soldiers by the strangeness of the sight, insomuch that, as if their limbs were paralysed, they (the soldiers) exposed their bodies to the weapons of the enemy without attempting to move,

until stirred into action

> by the earnest exhortations of the general.

As a consequence the Roman governor, Julius Agricola, began relentlessly suppressing the Druidic priesthood throughout England and Wales.

Agricola later sailed his 9th Legion into Morecambe Bay, and after subjugating the troublesome local Celts and eliminating their Druidic priests (including, presumably, those in the Setantii stronghold of Heysham) he moved inland to fortify the hilltop settlement of Longovieus (Lancaster). From there he marched his troops as far as southern Scotland where he vanquished the Caledonians in a mighty battle in 86 AD before receiving orders from Rome to withdraw. The Roman emperor Domitian is said to have been jealous of Agricola's military successes and worried by his growing popularity.

Evidence of Setantii presence at Heysham could once be found in the form of grinding bowls and other hollowed-out stones plundered from the Rectory Wood some years ago to be used as plant-pots in gardens around Heysham Village and beyond. These ancient stones appeared to have been re-used in the building of terraces upon which fruit and vegetables were grown in the 18th century. The feature known by tradition as the 'Druid Altar' has survived (along with its smaller companion) to testify to the importance of Heysham as a centre of Druidic worship, if indeed it is a genuine Druid altar.

'Druid Altar' in the Rectory Wood

In the beginning ...

A piece of ancient verse of doubtful meaning (possibly translated from Old English) which refers to Heysham's 'Druid Altar' claims:

> Whose hand but once upon the altar lay must farm the curse that ever lasts of those whose sinful price to pay.

Although the meaning of this may have been lost in translation and the verse itself generally forgotten, there were many old Heyshammers who never in their lives laid a hand upon the 'Druid Altar' - just in case ... !

With the Druidic priesthood eliminated throughout England and Wales and most of the country enjoying a period of relative peace, Roman strategy changed from offensive to defensive and in 120 AD the building of Hadrian's Wall began. Shortly afterwards the Roman settlers began to arrive, people of many different races from all over the Roman empire, Spain, Crete, Germany, Burgundy, the Middle East, etc.

The Romans founded cities and established a highly efficient centralized system of government in order to administer the affairs of a population estimated at around four million. Then into Britain came the early Christian missionaries to 'spread the word'. Many Celtic leaders, no longer under the influence of their maniacal priesthood, became closely allied with the Roman conquerors and were eventually converted to Christianity.

Some historians believe that a wooden structure once stood where Heysham's St Peter's Church now stands, and was used as a place of Christian worship as early as the 4th century AD.

During this period the Roman Empire flourished, but then began its slow yet inevitable decline as one by one its scattered provinces fell to rebellion or invasion. By 410 AD the Roman military contingents had been called back from Britain to deal with problems closer to the heart of the crumbling Empire, leaving the Romano-British population without military protection and open to attack by marauding barbarians.

St Patrick (c. 391-461 AD)

British by birth (the son of a Romano-British Christian family) St Patrick was enslaved as a child by Irish pirates who raided his home in the dying days of the Roman military occupation. As he grew towards manhood tending his master's herds he assimilated many Druidic elements into his existing Christian beliefs. Later, after converting his master and many of his fellow slaves, he and his followers, armed with a persuasive combination of Christianity and Paganism, evangelized the people of Ireland. First they had to overcome the reluctant worship of the fearsome god Crom Cruach, to whom the Celts of Ireland were obliged to offer the first fruits of their harvest and their first-born children.

--ooOoo--

2. *The Barbarians*

According to the Venerable Bede (c. 673-735 AD), a reclusive Northumbrian monk who is regarded generally as a reliable historian, England began to be settled by the Angles, the Saxons and the Jutes in the mid-5th century, although the Jutes, he claimed, settled mostly in Kent and the Isle of Wight.

Bede, who gave us the term 'England' ('Angle's land') claimed that the Angles and the Jutes came from the Danish peninsula, while the Saxons and other related tribes came from the German lowlands around the Rhine estuary. During the succeeding Anglo-Saxon epoch England became divided into a number of separate kingdoms. Various Saxon tribes dominated the eastern and southern areas, until finally the combined Saxon kingdom came to be known as Wessex after the more dominant West Saxons. Meanwhile warring Angles occupied independent regions throughout the rest of the country. Eventually the Anglian regions merged into three powerful kingdoms, Mercia (in the Midlands), Northumbria (which later included the whole of northern England from Yorkshire to the Scottish border), and East Anglia. (See map on page vi.)

With no form of central government neither the Angles nor the Saxons divided or apportioned land with a treaty and a handshake. For centuries the country was torn apart by warring rulers, greedy for more territory. Areas of land were mostly gained and held by force of arms, and it was firmly believed at the time that glory could only be achieved through warfare.

Although Northumbria had been occupied by Angles since c. 460 AD, later Anglo-Saxon records make no mention of kings or even tribal leaders during this early period. It was not until Saxon incursions into the north began that the first recorded kings of Northumbria appear, and these are found to be Saxon. In fact everything regarded as having been written by the 'Anglo-Saxons' was actually written in the language of the West Saxons.

The term 'Northumbria', when used to identify a geographical area in the 5th Century, applies strictly to the eastern side of the country between the Humber to the Firth of Forth. This region consisted of two major kingdoms, Bernicia (north of the Tees on both sides of the Roman wall), and Deira (in east Yorkshire), and several minor kingdoms, the names of which have been lost to history. Eventually most of these minor kingdoms were absorbed as the Saxon warrior king Ida and his offspring subjugated or expelled the Celtic population and imposed their rule over the Anglian settlers. Even then several independent Celtic kingdoms existed on the fringes of this territory, while a coalition of Celtic tribes continued to defend and to occupy the western side of the country from the River Severn to the Solway Firth for another two hundred years. It was not until Celtic resistance had ended that the first Anglian settlers began moving westward, reaching Heysham about the end of the 7th Century.

--ooOoo--

3. *The King of Britain*

Although the Celts of the north-west were divided by political differences and territorial frontiers, in their struggle against the Anglo-Saxon invaders they came to refer to themselves collectively as 'Kymry', which is believed to have meant 'comrades' or 'fellow countrymen'.

The term 'Kymry' (sometimes used to identify the Celts of the north-west in general) in its strictest sense appears to have had a military connotation and to have implied more specifically 'comrades-in-arms'. This confederation of military Celts owed its origin to the Roman policy of recruiting into military service the inhabitants of Roman provinces to assist in the defence of their native soil, and increasingly in later years to help defend other parts of the crumbling Roman Empire. As the last of the Roman legions withdrew from England these military Celts, who by now proudly served their Roman masters, were informed by the Supreme Commander of the Roman Army that the defence of their homeland was now in their own hands.

The Celtic military leader who inherited the office of Supreme Commander of the Army was the legendary Cunedda, king of the North, who features prominently in ancient Welsh literature. Cunedda is believed to have been the son of a daughter of King Coel who ruled the country of Ayr in the south-west of Scotland. (This is 'Old King Coel' of the nursery rhyme, not the later Coel of the West Saxons.)

Cunedda, although his name is Celtic, appears to have had a Roman father, so by virtue of his ancestry and his inherited military might he became over-king of all the Celts, a position which carried with it the title 'King of Britain'.

Cunedda's kingdom, which he ruled from his court in Carlisle, included part of southern Scotland, the whole of northern England, and the northern counties of Wales, and although many other independent kingdoms existed throughout England and Wales Cunedda's authority was accepted by all.

In the early years following the departure of the Romans, Cunedda appears to have been successful in defending the north of England against the Picts and the Scots, but his forces were less successful against the Anglian invaders from the east who soon began establishing settlements along the east coast.

Without assistance from the Roman army the rulers of the southern kingdoms were equally as unsuccessful in defending their territories against the Saxons. England's eastern coastline (known in Roman times as 'the Saxon Shores') had been heavily defended by the Romans who had successfully repulsed several Saxon invasions.

At one point Cunedda sent his sons into Wales to dispel raiders from Ireland who were attempting to establish settlements there, after which several of his sons remained in Wales where their descendants continued to rule various districts for many centuries. (It was once believed that Cunedda himself had been sent into Wales by the Romans, but this in now in doubt.)

Celtic kingdoms then were often divided into regional or sub-kingdoms, which meant that several kings may appear to have been ruling the same territory at the same time. Most of these 'kings', however, were tribal leaders subject to the rule of a regional over-king, who in turn obeyed the decrees of the 'King of Britain'.

Following the death of Cunedda the north of England broke up into a number of regional kingdoms, the rulers of which appear to have been, like Cunedda, either descended from King Coel or to have had some form of Roman ancestry. Instead of uniting to expel the Anglian invaders these regional rulers spent much of their time fighting each other for the right to inherit both Cunedda's old kingdom and the title 'King of Britain'. Cunedda's eldest son, who had remained with him in the north of England, is believed to have died before he could succeed, causing the break-up of the kingdom and the adoption of the title 'King of Britain' by the most powerful of the regional rulers, the king of Bernicia. This unknown king, in addition to dealing with regional uprisings and Pictish/Scottish incursions from the north, also had Anglian invaders to contend with.

Although gaining much territory as a result of these internal conflicts the Angles appear to have been unable to subjugate the Celts, so Bernicia and several other northern kingdoms remained in Celtic hands even when Saxon warrior kings were allegedly conquering the whole of Northumbria many years later.

A few words perhaps need to be said in order to distinguish between the Scots and the Picts. The term 'Picti' simply meant 'painted men'. These were the descendants of the northern Celts who were driven into Scotland by the Romans, or were already in Scotland at the time, before the Roman wall was built to contain them. The term 'Scotti' on the other hand implied 'scarred' or 'scored' men, and referred to those who engaged in the practice of tattooing (piercing the face and body with iron and injecting blue or purple dye into the wounds). This practice, which apparently originated in Ireland, set the Scotti apart from the other Irish Celts who drove them into the north-east corner of the country. Later, as a result of being continually harassed by their enemies, the Scotti fled across the sea to Scotland where they settled, eventually giving the country its name.

During the Roman occupation the English Celts abandoned the practice of painting their bodies, as testified by the fact that the term 'Picti' was used by both the Romans and the English Celts to denote only those Celts north of the Roman wall who continued the practice.

--ooOoo--

4. The Anglo-Saxon Wars

The Saxon chieftain Aella, after landing in England around 477, founded a colony on the Sussex coast and later established the kingdom of the South Saxons after beating the Celts in several major battles. Then, convinced that he was invincible, he arrogantly declared himself 'King of Britain'.

This was such an effrontery to the Celts it roused them to a state of national fury and incited them to combine their forces against him. At the time the Supreme Military Commander of the Britons was Ambrosius Aurelianus, a regional ruler of the southern kingdom of Dumnonia which consisted of Cornwall, Devon, Somerset and part of Dorset. Popularly known as 'the last of the Romans' Ambrosius led the Celtic forces to victory at the battle of Mount Badon in 519, and after several other major victories (all of which were later attributed to the seemingly mythical 'King Arthur') the Celts were able to halt the western expansion of the Saxons for several decades. Because of this, and possibly in view of the disputes that had been taking place in the north of England since the death of Cunedda, in the south of the country Ambrosius was regarded as 'the rightful King of Britain'.

The first recorded Anglo-Saxon king of the north appeared not long afterwards in 547, when the warrior chieftain Ida allegedly conquered the kingdom of Bernicia. Ida may in fact have been the leader of a band of Saxon mercenaries, 'hired' by the King of Bernicia to help him fight off his enemies, the Scots, the Picts, and the Anglian settlers who were edging their way further into Celtic territory. The practice of offering land to foreign mercenaries in exchange for military service appears to have been erroneously attributed by later Saxon historians to the mythical King Vortigern of Kent who is said to have offered land to Jutish mercenaries for just such a purpose. After driving off the invaders the Jutes allegedly turned against Vortigern and settled Kent themselves. Evidence suggests, however, that these events actually took place in Bernicia before the Jutes (led by Octha) had 'passed from the northern part of Britain to the region of the Cantii (Kent)', and from Octha (according to the British monk Nennius) arose the kings of the Cantii!

The term 'vortigern' appears to have referred to a Celtic 'over-king' and may be better expressed as *the* vortigern (the over-king of the Celts), a title claimed at the time by the powerful king of Bernicia.

The land granted to Ida and his followers was undoubtedly in the the south-east of Bernicia, but after subjugating the Anglian settlers and driving out many of the Celtic inhabitants, Ida, with support from his newly-conquered subjects, was able to extend his military might so far beyond the boundaries of his own lands that after conquering the Bernician stronghold of Bamburgh he laid claim to the whole kingdom. Meanwhile his son Aella had begun subjugating the people of the neighbouring kingdom of Deira.

--ooOoo--

5. *The Kymry*

As more and more territory fell to the Anglo-Saxons the term 'Kymry' came into being, perhaps as the warring Celts of the north-west of England and their similarly warring counterparts in North Wales remembered their traditional role as defenders of their native soil. Exactly when or how this came about will never be known. It can only be assumed that when the learned men of the north held one of their occasional meetings, at which matters of great importance were discussed and common policies decided upon, the attendant chieftains had no choice but to accept the fact that regardless of any previous political or territorial disputes they must now stand united against the common enemy, or perish!

Hitherto the inhabitants of Cumbria and Westmorland had independently resisted incursions from Bernicia, while the people of Lancashire, Cheshire and North Wales had dealt similarly with incursions from Deira, but now, when the Northumbrians began moving further into Celtic territory, the combined forces of the newly-formed Kymric alliance fiercely resisted and countered by launching destructive attacks on Anglian farming communities. This led to a period of continual warfare which appears to have come to end when both sides agreed to a truce that respected each other's territory and even allowed small Celtic tribal kingdoms to remain in the West Riding of Yorkshire.

The coveted title 'King of Britain' however, was still the cause of much dispute, so a powerful or charismatic figure was needed under whose leadership the disparate Celtic chieftains could unite. Into the picture at this point steps King Maelgwn, ruler of the kingdom of Gwynedd in North Wales, a direct descendant of the legendary Romano-British king Cunedda.

Maelgwn had become commander-in-chief of the Britons after the death of Ambrosious, and Welsh tradition tells how he then became over-king of the Celts when learned men from many parts of England and Wales assembled to decide who should be chief over them. Maelgwn was selected and invested with the title 'King of Britain', after which the title remained with the Cunedda family for several generations as Maelgwn's descendants succeeded each other as rulers of the kingdom of Gwynedd.

According to Celtic tradition the ruler of Bernicia at this time (twenty years after the Saxon chieftain Ida had allegedly conquered the kingdom) was the Celtic king Hussa, who reigned from 567 to 574 AD.

Aella, Ida's eldest son, had become ruler of the neighbouring kingdom of Deira in 560, while Ida's second son Ethelric succeeded his father as king of Bernicia in 568, a year after the reign of the Celtic king Hussa began.

How both Saxon and Celtic kings might be regarded as having ruled over the same kingdom at the same time is difficult to comprehend, but may be due to the fact that the Celts had been driven into the north of Bernicia where their kings (who are found only in Welsh tradition) probably still ruled. Later Anglo-Saxon 'historians', who recorded historical events with an Anglo-Saxon bias, may have chosen not to mention the existence of these Celtic rulers.

King Ethelric, who now ruled both Bernicia and Deira, led his forces into North Wales where he attacked and devastated the kingdom of Gwynedd. For what reason is not known, although it is a significant fact that the Celts of North Wales had recently joined the Kymric alliance, and Maelgwn had been invested with the title 'King of Britain', a title coveted not only by other Celtic rulers, but also by the most powerful of the Anglo-Saxon Kings.

In retaliation Maelgwn's son, Rhun, and the combined forces of the Kymry, launched a counter attack into Northumbria. There the Celtic King Hussa of Bernicia, instead of joining the Kymry to fight against the Northumbrians, is found to have fought against Urien, Rhydderch, and other Celtic leaders.

Hussa may in fact have been fighting on the side of Ethelric, either as a vassal king committed to military service in exchange for being allowed to rule over his own lands, or out of revenge for being denied by his own countrymen the right to inherit the title 'King of Britain', or both! The disputes between King Hussa and other Celtic rulers culminated in a great battle a few miles outside Carlisle in 573, after which Rhydderch fled to Dumbarton in Scotland (at that time the northernmost outpost of the English territories).

Urien, who ruled the area of northern England later known as Cumbria, appears again in conflict with Theodric, a later Celtic king of Bernicia, who is said to have ruled from 580 to 587. Urien was assassinated in 590 by his ally Morcant, who appears to have been jealous of the former's position as commander of the Kymric forces in the north of England.

Shortly afterwards a party of Irish missionaries (believed to have been disciples of St Columba) appear to have landed at Heysham where they are said to have erected a structure on the site of today's St Patrick's Chapel. From here they reconverted the local Celts, who by this time had abandoned most of their Christian traditions. This early form of Celtic Christianity, however, is said to have contained strong elements of paganism, as Columba's alleged statement 'Christ the Son of God is my Druid' appears to indicate.

St Columba (521-597 AD)
A Celtic monk

Born in the County of Donegal, Columba founded many monasteries in Ireland, then, in 563, accompanied by 12 other monks he sailed for Iona off the coast of Argyllshire in Scotland. There he established a monastery and began his missionary work, becoming known as 'the Apostle of the Highlands'. He and his followers embraced the doctrines of St Patrick and refused later to align them with those of the Roman Church. Heysham's Irish missionaries were once thought to have arrived direct from Ireland, but it now seems more-likely that they came from the monastery at Iona shortly before the death of St Columba, and later events indicate that the original 'St Patrick's Chapel' was regarded for some considerable time in the north-west of England as a symbol of Celtic Christianity. It appears to have been because of this that the 'chapel' was first destroyed, then later rebuilt by Benedictine monks from Northumbria after Celtic Christian practices had been aligned with those of the Roman Church.

Meanwhile King Ceawlin of the West Saxons was making further inroads into Celtic territories. He had defeated the Celts at Deorham in 577, taken Bath, Gloucester and Cirencester, invaded Shropshire and completely destroyed Shrewsbury. He was defeated, however, at Faddiley on the border of Cheshire in 584. In contrast the Kymry's vigorous defence of the north-west had led to a period of uneasy peace, but this situation was soon to change dramatically.

In Northumbria, after the death of Ethelric in 592, his brother Aelle reclaimed the kingdom of Deira, while Ethelfrith (the youngest brother) became king of Bernicia. Shortly afterwards in 596, as Heysham's Irish missionaries began spreading their brand of Christianity throughout the north-west of England, Augustine was sent from Rome to convert the Anglo-Saxons. He met with the learned men of the Kymry and asked them to assist him in converting the people of Northumbria, but angered by Augustine's arrogance and his intolerant attitude towards their form of Christianity the men of the Kymry refused.

St Augustine (c. 554-608 AD)
Prior of St Andrew's monastery in Rome

With 40 Benedictine monks he was sent to Britain by Pope Gregory I to convert the English. Landing on the Isle of Thanet he first converted Ethelbert king of Kent, whose queen, Bertha, was already a Christian. Within two years the entire population of Kent had been converted. Augustine's chief seat of worship was at Canterbury where he held regular services at the Church of St Martin, a relic of the Roman occupation. As more churches were built Augustine was made first Archbishop of Canterbury and Primate of Britain by Pope Gregory. The Celts of the north-west however, who had been Christianized by the followers of Columba, refused to accept Augustine's authority.

The Benedictines (or Black Monks)

Named after their founder (the Italian monk Benedict) and introduced into Britain by St Augustine, the Benedictines wore black habits and became known as the 'Black Monks'. The later Cistercians, in order to distinguish themselves from the Benedictines, chose to wear white. In England all cathedral priories and most of the great abbeys were Benedictine, and the Order, which became a powerful influence throughout the Dark Ages, was prominent in the field of scholarship and education. Many colleges, including five at Oxford and Cambridge, were founded by Benedictines. Lancaster Priory housed monks of the Benedictine Order, and in Norman times succeeding priors of Lancaster were 'lords' of the manor of Lower Heysham until the 15th Century.

Although historical evidence of the following events is scant, Ethelfrith is known to have invaded Deira in 604 (possibly after the death of Aelle) driving Aelle's young son Edwin into exile. Edwin appears to have found refuge with the Kymry of North Wales, where tradition has him residing in the kingdom of Gwynedd at the court of King Cadvan (over-king of the Celts) who had lived in peace with Edwin's father, King Aella, for some years.

In 613, on discovering Edwin's whereabouts, Ethelfrith (now king of the whole of Northumbria), afraid the exiled prince might one day return to claim his throne, marched his army from York towards the Welsh border in the hope of capturing Edwin. Expecting to meet strong resistance on reaching Celtic territory Ethelfrith rode at the head of the greatest Northumbrian army ever assembled. The Kymry, seeing this as a major invasion of their territory, gathered their combined forces at Chester and laid in wait for Ethelfrith and his advancing horde.

As Ethelfrith's mighty army reached Chester a great many British monks, accompanied by a detachment of Kymry, gathered at Bangor (on the Dee) to pray for the success of their Celtic brethren. On hearing of this the pagan king Ethelfrith dispatched a force of troops to slaughter the monks. The Kymry detachment sent to protect them fled when Ethefrith's troops arrived, leaving 1,200 monks to die by the sword. This incident was later regarded by the Anglo-Saxons as a judgement on the Kymry for rejecting Augustine's plea for assistance.

In the battle that followed, although Chester was cleared of its Celtic inhabitants, the slaughter was so great that neither side appears to have been able to claim complete victory. Both were so weakened that Anglo-Saxon tradition claims victory for the Northumbrians, while Welsh tradition claims likewise for the Kymry.

After the battle however, while the Kymry struggled to reorganize, Ethelfrith managed to push his depleted forces further west until they occupied the Wirral (the area between the River Dee and the Mersey), weakening the military might of the Kymry even more by splitting their forces in two.

Edwin then left Gwynedd and fled to East Anglia where he was granted refuge in the court of King Readwald. On discovering this Ethelfrith attempted several times to bribe Readwald to kill Edwin, but Readwald refused to comply. Ethelfrith then threatened him with war, but Readwald still refused, so Ethelfrith led his army into East Anglia where he was met by a great force led by Readwald and Edwin. In the ensuing battle Ethelfrith was slain and Edwin returned in triumph to his native Deira. As the rightful heir to the throne of Deira he then succeeded Ethelfrith as king of the whole of Northumbria and his military might soon won him the position of over-king of all the Saxons. All, that is, except the Christian King Ethelbert of Kent, the first Saxon king to be converted by Augustine.

Missionaries from Rome were hard at work by this time Christianizing the Saxons in the South. So Edwin, in order to ally his kingdom with the powerful kingdom of Kent, promised to become a Christian and married Ethelbert's devoutly Christian daughter. She then moved with him to York, followed by her bishop, Paulinus.

Conversion of an Anglo-Saxon to Christianity

It appears that Edwin had been married earlier to a daughter of his mortal enemy Ethelfrith (possibly in the hope of gaining acceptance as king of the whole of Northumbria after her father) but what became of her is not known. Along with other members of his court Edwin was baptised by Bishop Paulinus and became a Christian in 627. Then, as the bishop began the task of Christianizing the rest of the population of Northumbria, Edwin went to war on the Celts, attacking first the isolated Celtic kingdoms which still existed in parts of Northumbria. This action led to thirty years of devastating warfare between the Northumbrians and the allied forces of the Kymry.

In the South of the country during this period Saxon and Celtic kingdoms existed side by side. But the Celts of the South were not Kymry, and although the southern Celts had earlier fought against the Saxons it appears to have been the Kymry alone who had inherited from the Romans the commitment to defend Britain against the foreign invader. Since the time of King Maelgwyn it was the chief of the Kymry who had held the title 'King of Britain'. The most powerful of the Saxon rulers might become over-king of the Saxons, but none since the time of Aella of Sussex had dared risk infuriating the entire Celtic population by attempting to claim the title 'King of Britain'. None, that is, until the powerful and ambitious King Edwin decided that the title should be his.

Edwin's action against the Celts seems to have been the result of a dispute with Cadvan's son, King Cadwallon of Gwynedd. It had been the custom in Roman times for the military leader to carry before him a standard which bore a purple dragon, and this practice appears to have been inherited by the kings of the Kymry, many of whom, like the Cunedda family, were of Roman descent.

The leaders of the Kymry cherished these traditions and proudly wore other insignia inherited from the Romans under whom their ancestors had served. Cadwallon had refused to agree when Edwin requested the right to celebrate the same festivals and to bare the same emblems in his own kingdom that Cadwallon did in his. The only way to settle the matter, as far as Edwin was concerned, was to take 'the Crown of Britain' from Cadwallon by force of arms. Edwin then went to war against the Kymry in general, and the kingdom of Gwynedd (his former sanctuary) in particular.

Earlier King Ethelfrith, when marching his mighty army from York to Chester, appears to have peacefully bypassed the Celtic kingdoms in the West Riding of Yorkshire, so Edwin's surprise invasion gained him an easy victory. He immediately annexed these kingdoms to his own kingdom of Northumbria and then led his forces westwards to the sea, splitting the Kymry in two once again and pushing them into two separate areas.

It has been said that after the Battle of Chester the Kymry went scampering off into the north of England destroying everything along the way to delay pursuit, 'including the little Christian colony based around St Patrick's Chapel'.

Directly after the battle, however, Ethelfrith seems to have been too preoccupied with the capture of Edwin to risk sending his depleted forces any further into Celtic territory than the Wirral. The

St Patrick's Chapel

Kymry may indeed be said to have been 'torn in two' at this time, but only until Ethelfrith left the Wirral to continue his pursuit of Edwin.

The Kymry, it seems, continued to occupy the northwest of England (including Lancashire) until Edwin's invading forces divided them again and pushed them into the areas which still bear their name - Cumbria (in the north of England), and Cambria (North Wales). The structure which stood where 'St Patrick's Chapel' now stands appears to have been destroyed around this time.

The Kymry, who had so far refused to accept the authority of the Roman Church, still embraced the doctrines of St Patrick.

It seems reasonable for Edwin to have assumed therefore, that with both the military might and the political power of the Kymry severely weakened the only thing holding them together was their common religion. For a time the monastery at Bangor on the Dee had been an important centre of Kymric Christianity, but the monastery had been destroyed earlier by Ethelfrith and his forces. Now only Heysham's Celtic Christian structure remained.

Although not a monastery, this building is unlikely to have been a 'chapel' in the accepted sense of the term. A chapel is a small or subordinate place of Christian worship (other than a parish or cathedral church) erected for private or semi-public devotion, and the term is usually applied to places of nonconformist worship. The term 'chapel', therefore, can only apply to the existing St Patrick's Chapel, rebuilt by Anglian missionaries and subordinate to their own (St Peter's) church. The original building appears to have been of far greater importance, being regarded by both the Celts and the Northumbrians as the very symbol of Kymric Christianity, the place from which Columba's disciples spread their Christian message throughout the north-west of England.

With these centres of Kymric Christianity destroyed, the doctrines of the Roman Church could be introduced and the Kymric alliance might then begin to crumble as individual loyalties became confused.

However, the spirit of Kymric resistance was not so easily broken. Although the inhabitants of Heysham and the surrounding area appear to have been wholly at the mercy of Edwin (whose conquests included the Isle of Man), the Kymry later continued their activities against the Northumbrians from their two new strongholds of Cumbria and North Wales, sometimes separately and sometimes together. Unfortunately the names of most of the warrior kings of the north of England and the traditions associated with them were lost when the region later became populated by Anglo-Saxons and the Celtic language faded out of existence. In Wales on the other hand, which was never conquered by the Anglo-Saxons, the language survived and many Kymric traditions survived with it, passing later into Welsh.

Welsh tradition speaks of the area along the west coast of England, which the Angles of Northumbria eventually occupied, as reaching from the River Dee to the forests of Cumberland and the neighbourhood of Derwent. The occupation of this territory, however, appears to have taken place over a long period of time, continuing for many years after the first Anglian settlers arrived at Heysham. The westward onslaught of Edwin and his forces failed to open the territory to Anglian settlers at this time.

--ooOoo--

6. *The Kymric Revival*

With the Kymry now divided and their military might weakened, Edwin (after destroying the traditional home of Kymric religion at Heysham) led his army south towards the kingdom of Gwynedd, allowing Heysham's dispirited inhabitants to return to their farms to carry on with their lives as before.

If we can accept the term 'Kymry' as having had a military connotation we must therefore consider the fact that in any society not everyone is a member of the armed forces. Like the Angles and the Saxons, the Celts were basically farmers, and even in these turbulent times many farmers would have remained on (or quickly returned to) their own land to continue ploughing and planting and harvesting. The infrastructure of the various Celtic kingdoms throughout the whole of Britain depended upon food production; and now there were the Kymric forces to feed. In some cases an army might survive by foraging, but not when Kymric forces were defending Kymric territory. To ravage the land would be to destroy a delicately balanced system that had taken hundreds of years to develop.

The Anglo-Saxons on the other hand, who employed an early form of feudalism (the allotting of land in exchange for a commitment to military service), would have operated by different criteria.

Although the Kymry had retreated from Lancashire to reorganize and to fight elsewhere, Celtic farmers and their families, who may have been driven from their homes during the initial onslaught of Edwin's Northumbrian forces, would almost certainly have returned to their homes when Edwin and his army left to wage war on Cadwallon. In fact after Edwin's death the situation altered completely, with Cadwallon and the Kymry virtually ruling the whole of Northumbria.

After several battles (the names of which have been lost) Cadwallon was forced into exile in Ireland, so Edwin, satisfied now that the 'Crown of Britain' was his, left Gwynedd and returned to his own kingdom of Northumbria. Around this time Edwin became known by the title 'Brytenwealder' ('wielder' or 'ruler' of Britain), a title which for some time afterwards applied only to the powerful kings of Northumbria. This title, although the Anglo-Saxon equivalent of the Celtic 'King of Britain', failed to incite the entire Celtic population to rise against him. Not so, however, with the Anglian king Penda of Mercia.

Penda, Edwin's nearest neighbour, had firmly established the independence of Mercia by beating the Saxons at Cirencester in 628 and was fanatically determined to maintain his independence. Worried now by the fast-growing power of King Edwin, Penda began to invade Northumbria.

On hearing of this Cadwallon returned from Ireland, and after re-assembling the

Kymric forces he formed an alliance with the warrior king Penda. The combined forces of the Kymry and the Mercians then began waging all-out war on Northumbria until, in 633, Edwin was finally defeated and killed at Hadfield Chase near Doncaster.

Cadwallon and the Kymry then marched into Northumbria and took York, the seat of the kingdom of Deira, where they were soon besieged by Edwin's son Osric, but Osric was killed and his forces scattered when the Kymry launched a sudden counter-attack.

Then Ethelfrith's son Enfrith returned to claim the kingdom of Bernicia. Enfrith had been in exile in Scotland during the reign of Edwin and had married a Pictish princess, but he returned on hearing of Edwin's death. Cadwallon then marched his Kymric forces into Bernicia, and with reinforcements from Cumbria drove Enfrith and his army northwards towards Scotland. Enfrith was overtaken, however, and was killed in battle at Hexham near Hadrian's Wall. He had ruled Bernicia for one year only, from 633 to 634.

When Cadwallon was finally killed in 635 by Enfrith's brother Oswald (who then became king of the whole of Northumbria), Cadwallon's son Cadwallar and the Kymric forces maintained their alliance with King Penda and the war with Northumbria continued. Eight years later, after Oswald had been killed in battle, Bernicia and Deira once again became two separate kingdoms.

King Oswald of Northumbria (605-642 AD)

Oswald (another son of Ethelfrith) had fled into exile on the Isle of Iona when Edwin became king of Bernicia, and while at Iona he became a Christian in the Celtic tradition (popularly referred to as the 'British' tradition). On hearing of the death of his brother Enfrith he returned to Bernicia where he continued the war against the Kymry, and after defeating Cadwallon he became king of Northumbria. He then summoned the Celtic monk Aidan from Iona and gave him the island of Lindisfarne. For his part in re-establishing Christianity in Northumbria (albeit of the Celtic variety) Oswald became the first Anglo-Saxon king to be canonized. In the light of this it can only be assumed that the Roman bishop Paulinus, although having earlier converted Edwin and other members of his court, had failed to convert Edwin's Northumbrian subjects. Either that, or during the many years of disruptive warfare with the pagan king Penda and the Kymry, the Northumbrians had reverted to the worship of their old gods.

After Oswald's death his son Oswin and his brother Oswy (Ethelfrith's third son) contested the succession, so Northumbria became divided again with Oswy ruling the kingdom of Bernicia and Oswin ruling Deira. Nine years of peace followed until, in 651, Oswy murdered his nephew Oswin and united the two kingdoms again. This prompted Penda and the Kymry to launch such a devastating attack on Northumbria that Oswy and his forces were driven into Scotland where the Northumbrian king found refuge in Edinburgh (originally 'Edwin's Burgh', Northumbria's most northern outpost). The beleaguered King Oswy then offered Penda all the riches he had in his possession if he would remain within the boundaries of his own kingdom and cease his activities against Northumbria.

Penda appears to have accepted these gifts and distributed them amongst the leaders of the Kymry who accompanied him. Then he continued the war! He was finally killed by the Northumbrians shortly afterwards, either at 'the slaughter of Gai's Field' or at the Battle of Winwead near Leeds where Oswy is said to have ended the war in 655 after most of the warrior chieftains of the Kymry had fallen and the spirit of Kymric resistance had been finally broken.

Oswy then rose to great power ruling Mercia and much of Southern Scotland in addition to Northumbria. He allowed his daughter Alchfled, to marry Penda's son Peada, on condition that he became a Christian. Later in 664, he presided over the Synod hosted by his cousin Hilda (Hild), Abbess of Whitby, at which representatives of the Celtic and Roman Churches met to establish a common formula for Christian worship.

Hilda, who had founded a double monastery at Whitby in 657 (housing both monks and nuns), favoured Celtic practices, her own monastery being organized after the rule of Columba. Oswy, however, appears to have been strongly influenced by the doctrines and practices of the Roman Church through the members of his court, in particular his friend and adviser, Benedict Biscop.

--ooOoo--

Whitby Abbey

7. A New Dawn

At the Whitby Synod Oswy's governing influence resulted in Celtic practices being aligned with those of the Roman Church, and although Hilda preferred the traditional British (Celtic) practices, she accepted the ruling of the Synod and reorganized her own monastery accordingly. Cuthbert, a Celtic prior who also accepted the reformation, became prior of Lindisfarne.

The Church of Iona, which later became the official Church of Scotland, refused to acknowledge the authority of the Roman Church, so the Christian practices of the Scots continued in accordance with the Rule of Columba. This effectively broke all connection between the Scottish and the English Churches. Just how long the isolated Celtic communities along the north-west coast of England continued to embrace Columba's doctrines is not known, but Celtic practices appear to have survived at least until the arrival of the first Anglian settlers and their accompanying missionaries. The architect of the reformation, or at least the major influence behind it, appears to have been the hitherto little-known Benedict Biscop.

Benedict Biscop (c. 629-689 AD)

Benedict, a Northumbrian of noble descent, spent his early life at the court of King Oswy, during which time he visited Rome on several occasions. He then became a monk and used his influence to turn Oswy away from his family's religious preferences to the doctrines and practices of the Roman Church. He later persuaded Oswy to preside over the all-important Synod at Whitby, and after Oswy's death in 670 Benedict was appointed abbot of St Peter's monastery at Canterbury. He returned to Rome several times, bringing back with him each time a vast number of books and manuscripts. He then founded a monastery at Wearmouth on land given to him by King Egfrith and created a huge library there. After further trips to Rome he founded a dependent monastery at Jarrow, apparently for the purpose of extending his library, the largest in the whole of Christendom.

The Venerable Bede lived most of his life in the monastery at Jarrow where he spent his time 'learning, teaching and writing'. In his teens he studied under Benedict Biscop and then under his successor Ceolfrid. While there he wrote his *Ecclesiastical History*, the main source of knowledge of early English history, derived mostly from the works of Roman writers and from English tradition. The first Anglian settlers arrived at Heysham during Bede's lifetime.

When settling an area Anglian missionaries would first erect an elaborately carved cross around which the congregation would gather while the ecclesiastic delivered his sermon. This practice would continue until a church had been built to house the congregation. Parts of such a cross and the church's original Anglian doorway are still in evidence at Heysham (the once-sacred heart of the religion of the legendary Kymry).

The sermons of the day appear to have been delivered by Benedictine monks from the monasteries of Jarrow or Wearmouth, and to have been aimed not so much at the Northumbrian settlers, but at the local population and their religious leaders in an attempt to persuade them to accept the doctrines and practices of the Roman Church.

The original Anglian doorway of St Peter's Church

St Patrick's Chapel was then built on the site of the earlier structure, apparently for use by those Celts who found some initial difficulty in fully accepting the reformation.

--ooOoo--

Anglian cross base in St Peter's churchyard

8. *Home of Hesse*

It has been suggested that Heysham would possibly have been occupied by no more than a small community of Anglian settlers. Hesse, their leader, probably lived with his family on the Barrows, and when not out hunting or fishing would have spent his time fighting off marauding brigands and protecting the community from all manner of assorted dangers, until eventually his name became known throughout the entire region. All newcomers to the area were then forewarned to stay well clear of the 'Home of Hesse'.

A modern-day US TV adventure series would undoubtedly present British history in this manner, but in the real world of the early 8th Century this is unlikely to have been the case. Anglian farming communities were no doubt encouraged to move west in order to extend the borders of Northumbria as far as possible into Celtic territory, but with the war between the Northumbrians and the Kymry only recently ended, even with a new and conciliatory age dawning, Anglian settlers heading west would have been venturing into unknown and possibly hostile territory. With the north-west being still occupied by Celts, and with so much resentment felt towards the Northumbrians who throughout living memory had been the traditional enemy of the Kymry, it is difficult to imagine Anglian peasant-farmers attempting to settle anywhere on the west coast without the protection of experienced fighting men. At least not until the two sides had become reconciled by evangelizing monks from Wearmouth or Jarrow.

Although Celtic religious practices had recently been aligned with those of the Roman Church this reformation is unlikely to have been immediately accepted by the inhabitants of isolated Celtic settlements in the north-west. The Benedictines, of course, would be eager to address this situation as quickly as possible, so the first Anglian settlers to venture west would almost certainly have been protected by warriors and accompanied by monks whose sole purpose would be to preach the doctrines of the Roman Church from the traditional home of Kymric Christianity at Heysham. In fact the rebuilding of 'St Patrick's Chapel' and the very existence at Heysham of such features as the 'Anglian Cross' and the original St Peter's Church testify to the presence of Benedictine monks and associated builders and craftsmen.

At that time Anglian families lived in humble dwelling of wood and thatch. Only 'the Church' was built in stone! Without the building skills of the Church these structures could not have been erected. The immediate efforts of Heysham's first Anglian settlers would have been devoted solely to the task of staying alive until the land had been ploughed and planted and harvested. Men of the Church on the other hand would have been supported by the entire community while the building of their religious structures was in progress.

A recent topographic survey carried out at Heysham concluded that elements of an important ecclesiastical complex similar to the monastic establishments at Jarrow and Wearmouth could be found around St Peter's Church and St Patrick's Chapel. This adds a little more potency to the belief that Heysham may once have been a place of far greater importance than has previously been suspected.

Possible evidence of an ecclesiastical complex

St Peter's Church was possibly so-named because Benedict Biscop (the founder of the monasteries at Jarrow and Wearmouth) had previously been the abbot of St Peter's monastery at Canterbury. St Patrick's Chapel obviously acquired its name by association. The disciples of Columba who erected the original structure had, of course, preached the doctrines of St Patrick.

If this was the case, then who was Hesse and why does the area still bear his name when all else about Heysham has been long forgotten? Most of the surrounding settlements, Poulton, Middleton, Overton, Heaton and so on, bear Saxon names, so how did the Anglian Hesse acquire such lasting fame that his name survived the later period?

The name Hesse is believed by some to have originated in Germany where it exists to this day in relation to a geographical area, and may therefore have been a tribal name rather than the name of an individual warrior as is generally supposed. Dr Andrew White (Curator of Lancaster City Museum) claims on the other hand that Heysham is an Anglian naming, perhaps of the 7th Century, and probably includes a personal name.

One opinion claims that Hesse was an important warrior chieftain who was chosen by King Aldfrith ('a statesman and a man of learning') to accompany and to protect the party of evangelizing monks on their journey to Heysham.

Back in Northumbria Hesse would possibly have been a major landowner, hence his chieftainship of a band of feudal warriors. The term 'home of Hesse' may have been used by later Anglian settlers to identify the area.

As for the predictable image of Hesse living with his family on Heysham Barrows, one or two other avenues may need to be explored before this idyllic scenario can be accepted.

Although Heysham's earliest inhabitants had made their home on the Barrows in Palaeolithic times, these people were hunter-gatherers, not farmers. Neither the location of the Barrows nor the land itself would have seemed quite so desirable to the chieftain of an Anglian farming community. In most respects the location of the Barrows with the breath-taking view from Chapel Hill is splendid, but if the warrior chieftain Hesse was important enough to leave his name to the area he would most certainly have chosen for himself a more suitable area of land than that which the small, wind-swept hillside now known as 'Heysham Barrows' had to offer. The monks themselves may have farmed the Barrows, which was adjacent to their ecclesiastical complex. When fishing they would no doubt have launched their tiny craft from their newly-built stone causeway that now lies forgotten on the edge of the little bay beside Throbshaw Point. (This land belonged to the Church for many years.)

In other parts of Heysham, however, far more suitable land for farming existed than that which could be found on the Barrows, although after so many years of housing development this may not be immediately apparent. The area between Cross Cop and the Battery (inland towards Oxcliffe) was once good, flat, arable farm land. To the right of Oxcliffe Road and beyond, past Heysham Moss and on towards Middleton and Heaton, many more acres of rich farming and grazing land still exist.

The preoccupation with Heysham Barrows is understandable as it was home to some of Britain's earliest inhabitants, and here the most important of such sites in the entire country was discovered in 1992[†]. The archaeologists concluded:

> The headland at Heysham is in excess of 100 hectares and only 12 square metres were excavated. The large number of artefacts recovered from such a small trench may well indicate that the headland was a major hunting centre during the Mesolithic period.

> The infertility of the soils would perhaps have led to the abandonment of the site when economic activity changed to settled farming.

> The intensity of occupation and evidence suggesting on-site manufacture of tools from imported raw materials leads the excavators to conclude that Heysham Head was a large and permanently occupied site throughout the whole of the Mesolithic period.

Hand in glove with the often disconcerting preoccupation with Heysham Barrows is the myopic view of Heysham itself which tends to disregard anything that may have taken place outside the confines of the village. The area of land occupied by Heysham's Anglian settlers most likely equated with that of Heysham today, stretching from the present-day Battery to the border of Middleton, and inland to the borders of Heaton and Oxcliffe. Much of this land would have also been farmed originally by Celts.

[†] C R Salisbury and D Sheppard : *The Mesolithic Occupation of Heysham Head* : 1994 Transactions of Lancashire & Cheshire Antiquarian Society Vol. 87 pp. 141-9

--ooOoo--

9. The Kings of Heysham

After the departure of the Romans, when Cunedda's mighty kingdom had broken up into smaller regional kingdoms, the king of Bernicia appears to have ruled most of the land of the Brigantes on the eastern side of the country both north and south of the Roman wall, while the western side of the country south of the wall was ruled by the king of Rheged.

Although the kingdom of Rheged is usually identified with Cumbria (to which it may have been later reduced), from his court at Carlisle the king of Rheged appears to have ruled the country from Solway Firth to the border of North Wales. This kingdom included, of course, the Setantii settlement later to become known as Heysham.

Named after the ancient Celtic Kingdom, Rheged is Cumbria's newest and largest visitor attraction.

Extract from the Rheged Centre brochure.
New Discovery Centre in Penrith, opened in 2000.

The first recorded king of Rheged is Owain, about whom little is known. Like Cunedda he appears to have been a Romano-British descendant of King Coel. He was succeeded by Urien (son of Cynfach) of the same royal household. As noted earlier Urien fought with the Kymry against both the Anglo-Saxon and Celtic Bernicians as they attempted to expand their territories towards the west.

The Kymry appear to have been descended from the Brythonic Celts found mostly in Cumbria, North and West Wales and Cornwall. In addition to attempting to halt the western expansion of the Bernicians and the later Northumbrians they often had cause to defend their territory against Celts of the Goidelic branch who occupied South Wales, Devon, Ireland, the Isle of Man and the Scottish Highlands. Welsh tradition tells of Urien and the Kymric coalition on one occasion waging war on the Goidelic Celts of South Wales, who were attempting to expand their territory northwards. Whether or not these considerations played any part in the conflict between King Hussa and the other regional rulers of the north is uncertain.

While four Celtic kings are known to have been opposed to the rule of King Hussa they are found also to have fought against each other in a continuing bid for power after the break-up of Cunedda's kingdom. These conflicts culminated in the battle of Arderydd (or Arfderydd) in 573 AD at the Knows of Artheret about 9 miles from Carlisle, a significant location as many of those involved appear in the later Arthurian legends. It is possibly because of this later infusion of history and legend that these events are given little consideration from a historical point of view. On the other hand it may be because ancient writers, after the Crown of Britain had passed to the Saxon rulers of the south, seem to have developed a perverse compulsion to relocate in the south of the country events which actually took place in the north.

Although Jutish settlers are believed to have landed near Ramsgate in Kent around 450 AD (perhaps under Hengist and Horsa) the fusing together, by later Anglo-Saxon historians, of these events and those in which the king of Bernicia appears to have been involved, may be seen as an example of this relocation of northern tradition.

Rhyderrch ap Tudwal, named as one of the four kings opposed to King Hussa of Bernicia, is known to most historians simply as the king of Dumbarton. He did not become king of Dumbarton, however, until after the battle of Arderydd, and although his original kingdom is not known his move to Dumbarton suggests that it lay somewhere in the area held by English Celts north of the Roman wall.

Rhyderrch re-established himself at Dumbarton after apparently losing his own kingdom to King Hussa, although he is said to have first defeated King Gwenddolau, to whom the historical Merlin (or Myrddyn) acted as bard and soothsayer. Merlin, who had prophesied victory for Gwenddolau, went insane when Gwenddolau and his forces were slaughtered. In his madness he remained for a while on a barren hillside near Carlisle, then wandered further north where he lived for some time in a cave. The madness of Merlin appears in several traditional stories and is attested by some historical evidence.

Exactly who was fighting who at the battle of Arderydd and who emerged victorious is not clear, although Urien, king of Rheged (called by his bard 'King of the Golden North'), is known to have survived to continue waging war on the Bernicians. Later he became too powerful and was assassinated while out on a campaign in 590. He was succeeded by his son, Owain (named after Urien's predecessor), who continued to fight with the Kymry against the Angles of Bernicia. It was during the reign of Owain, king of the north-west and a descendant of 'Old King Coel', that the disciples of St Columba commenced their missionary work from their newly-built oratory at Heysham. Northumbria at the time was ruled by King Ethelric.

Although the legendary King Arthur is said to have been mortally wounded at the battle of Camlan in 537 AD, Rhydderch, Urien, Merlin, and others involved in the battle of Arderydd, which took place in 573 (36 years after the battle of Camlan), appear as central figures in the later Arthurian legends. Even Urien's son, Owain, who succeeded him in 590, appears as the hero of several stories.

According to the Arthurian legends Urien was king of the land of Gore. He married Morgan le Fay who later bore him a son, Owain. In earlier versions of the legend Morgan le Fay (here called Modron) promised always to aid Urien and his family in the shape of a raven (the sacred bird of the Celts). Urien left Modron to become a Round Table Knight and was later killed while fighting with Arthur against Mordred. In reality he was killed by his ally Morcant while supporting the British cause (later symbolized by the mythical figure of Arthur). Many early Arthurian legends, it seems, were loosely based upon the memory of some ancient historical event, while Arthur himself appears to be a composite figure embodying the characteristics of several Celtic or Romano-British warrior chieftains.

Urien's son, Owain, is the hero of two Arthurian legends, 'The Lady of the Fountain' and 'The Dream of Rhonabwy'. In the latter he appears as Yvain in medieval versions of the story.

Although the historical Merlin was associated with the historical King Gwenddalau, his legendary association with the mythical King Arthur is too well known to require mention here. Less well known, perhaps, is the marriage of Merlin's wife, Guendolena, to Rhydderch ap Tudwal after the battle of Arderydd. The historical Rhydderch, after passing into legend, can be found as 'Rhydderch Hael' who owned a special sword named Dyrnwyn that flamed like fire when unsheathed (shades of Excalibur); and also as 'Rhydderch the Generous', who possessed a magic cauldron from which any number of heroes could be fed.

Because the Dumnonii people occupied two separate areas, one north of the Roman wall in the country of King Rhydderch, and one in the south which became the kingdom of Dumnonia, northern traditions relating to British resistance to the Anglo-Saxons were relocated in the south and, as a result of the later writings of Geoffrey of Monmouth, down south went the historical kings of the north-west to become mythical Arthurian heroes and rulers of mythical territories.

--ooOoo--

10. Heysham's New Inhabitants

In 793 AD the Viking raids began. The first recorded raid took place in the remote coastal area of Northumbria when Danish Vikings ruthlessly sacked and destroyed the Lindisfarne monastery.

After plundering England's defenceless coastal villages for more than 70 years the first full-scale Viking invasions began, and by 867 the Danish 'great army' had overrun East Anglia and Northumbria.

When the Vikings invaded Wessex during the time of Alfred the Great (871-899), Alfred defeated the Danish army at Edington and as a result the Viking king Guthrum agreed to leave Wessex and become a Christian. He and his army were allowed to settle and to control an area of eastern England that was to become known as 'Danelaw'.

Later victories over the Norwegian invaders at the close of the 9th century led to more Vikings becoming permanent residents in the country they had come to plunder. The Norwegians had already established a base in Ireland in 841, and from there had begun to colonize Northumbria's remote western coastal areas of Lancashire and Cumbria.

Beginning with Alfred the Great much of England was ruled from the south by the Saxon kings of Wessex and, although many independent kingdoms remained, the affairs of most regions were administered by members of an Anglo-Saxon aristocracy. These were powerful and wide-spread families who, on the king's behalf, taxed the land and everything it produced. However in the scattered and often isolated settlements of Northumbria southern influence proved difficult to impose and even more difficult to maintain. In 875 Halfran (Ragnarson) founded the independent kingdom of York which had thirteen Norse rulers in fifty years.

By the time the Norwegians arrived at Heysham the Celts had already been absorbed by the Anglo-Saxons who lived in modest dwellings of wood and turf and scratched out a meagre living from the land. The incoming Norwegians on the other hand made their living from the sea, and consequently the old fishing families of Morecambe are believed to be their direct descendants.

The 'hogback' stone, which stood originally in the grounds of St Peter's

Hogback stone, facing west

Church but is now inside the church, is of Viking origin and dates from this period. It was most likely placed over the grave of some Viking notable.

The rock-hewn graves on Chapel Hill indicate an entirely different burial practice. Although not unique, these graves have so far defied all attempt to date accurately.

Hollowed-out stone buried or cut level with the ground in which crosses were placed at the heads of important persons appear to reflect Scandinavian burial practices, although the overall design of this particular feature is somewhat unusual and all information relating to it is speculative.

--ooOoo--

Rock-hewn graves by St Patrick's Chapel

11. The Danes

The successors of Alfred the Great attempted to tighten their hold on the country and began taking back areas under Viking control, but while being successful to some extent in the east and the midlands they were once again less successful in the north. According to the *Anglo-Saxon Chronicle* the Danish chiefs of Northumbria conspired with the North and West Welsh, the Scots, and the Irish Norsemen (led by Analf), to overthrow the Saxon king Athelstan the Glorious, son of Edward, and replace him with a Northumbrian king. The Norwegians, Scots and Welsh are believed to have gathered at the Isle of Man and from there sailed across to the west coast of England, landing at a place called Brunenburh. King Athelstan arrived and a battle raged for two days before the invaders finally took to their ships and sailed away.

The actual location of 'the Battle of Brunenburh' cannot be determined from the account given in the *Anglo-Saxon Chronicle*, although some believe it to have taken place in the vicinity of Heysham's present-day Nuclear Power Stations. In 13th-Century Manor Court documents the term 'Bronneburh' appears in reference to a rock at Heysham and is cited as a boundary marker (probably the 'Big Stone' which marked the coastal boundary of the manor), while the terms 'Bruneberh' and 'Bruneberk' appear in reference to an area of land in the same vicinity. Although no physical evidence exists to indicate that this event took place at Heysham, other suggested sites suffer equally from a lack of evidence.

At least Heysham can boast the term 'Bronneburh', and strategically speaking the location of the area makes it an ideal site. With the Norwegians on the coast, their allies sailing up the Lune and attacking from the east, and the Northumbrians moving in from the north, Athelstan's army would have been completely surrounded.

Why such a strategy should have failed is a matter for military analysts. Until some physical evidence is uncovered however, this event cannot be honestly regarded as a part of the history of Heysham.

After another Danish uprising led by Erik Bloodaxe in 957 a period of peace followed allowing King Edgar (959 - 970 AD), Athelstan's nephew, to introduce sweeping religious reforms, and by the middle of the 10th century much of the country was being governed by a widespread Christianized uniform administrative system. Then the Vikings returned!

The Danes, under their king Sweyn Forkbeard, once again mounted full-scale attacks on England. The English king Ethelred 'the Unready', afraid of being caught between invading Danes on one hand and an uprising of English-resident Danes on the other, ordered the massacre of a great many resident Danes.

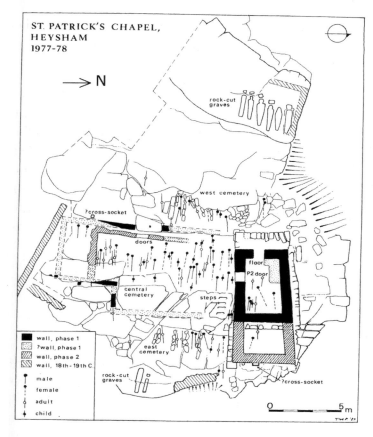

ST. PATRICK'S CHAPEL,
HEYSHAM
1977-78

→ N

rock-cut graves

west cemetery

?cross-socket

doors

floor

P2 door

central cemetery

steps

east cemetery

rock-cut graves

?cross-socket

wall, phase 1
?wall, phase 1
wall, phase 2
wall, 18th-19th C.
male
female
adult
child

0 — 5 m

St Patrick's Chapel and cemetery

General plan of the excavations

reproduced from

T W Potter and R D Andrews : *Excavation and Survey at St Patrick's Chapel and St Peter's Church, Heysham, 1977-78* : Antiquaries Journal Vol LXXIV 1994

Although Danes are known to have spread throughout the whole of Northumbria, predictably no evidence exists of Danish presence at Heysham. In 1977 however, an archaeological dig inside and around the ruins of St Patrick's Chapel uncovered the skeletal remains of about 80 persons of both sexes and of various ages, including children. Some skeletons were headless, and all appeared to have been roughly buried in shallow graves. Amongst the remains a 'Viking-age' comb was found.

Carbon dating of the bones, which were in generally poor condition, indicated that the bodies had been buried 'during the latter part of the 10th Century'. As ever this penetrating archaeological investigation into Heysham's ancient past turned out to be as vague and inconclusive as all the rest, and merely invites more speculation.

The massacre of the Danes led to an uprising in the Danelaw in 1013 which drove Ethelred into exile in Normandy with his Norman wife, Emma, and their two children, Alfred and Edward. Sweyn Forkbeard then became uncrowned king of England.

Ethelred returned after Sweyn's death, but found that Sweyn's son Canute had taken his father's place. When Ethelred died soon afterwards, Canute agreed to divide the country between himself and Ethelred's eldest son, Edmund Ironsides (with Canute ruling Mercia and Northumbria), but when Edmund was mysteriously assassinated later the same year Canute quickly established himself as king of all England.

In order to secure his kingship Canute married Ethelred's widow, Emma, who later bore him two sons, Harold (Harefoot) and Hardicanute.

Canute (who was also king of both Denmark and the recently conquered Norway) chose to rule his dominions from England where he officially abolished the various independent kingdoms and divided the country into four great earldoms. He gave Wessex to his English protégé, Godwine of the West Saxons, who was married to Canute's sister-in-law. As one of Canute's most powerful supporters Godwine had secured for himself a commanding position amongst the Anglo-Danish aristocracy.

On the death of Canute his son Harold (Harefoot) succeeded to the throne of England. He was succeeded in turn by his brother, Hardicanute, who was not suited to kingship and suffered from failing health.

After much court wrangling initiated by the powerful and scheming Earl Godwine, Hardicanute was persuaded to ask his step-brother Edward (son of Ethelred and Emma) to return to England. Edward (who soon became known as Edward 'the Confessor' because of his monk-like piety) became King when Hardicanute died in 1042 after ruling for only two years.

Edward then married Edith, daughter of Earl Godwine, who by now had become so powerful he was said by many to have 'ruled the King'. Edward, however, appears not to have been so easily ruled as Godwine had hoped. He invited young Normans to England to serve as his personal knights, and began appointing Norman noblemen to high positions at his court, weakening Godwine's position and presenting a threat to his personal ambitions. On more than one occasion the disputes between Edward and Earl Godwine almost resulted in civil war. Finally, because Edward and Edith remained childless, Edward made William of Normandy (to whom he was indirectly related through his mother, Emma) heir to the throne of England. This move was met with fierce opposition from Earl Godwine and his son Harold (King Edward's brother-in-law) who had long been regarded as the one most likely to succeed to the throne.

--ooOoo--

12. The first 'Lords' of Heysham

In 1055, after the death of the Danish Earl Siward of Northumbria who had defeated King Macbeth of Scotland, Harold's brother Tostig was made Earl of Northumbria.

In addition to administering the King's affairs throughout his earldom, like all chief administrators Tostig held many areas of land in his own right. One of these areas, of which Heysham was a part, was said to 'belong to Halton'.

Tostig, who ruled his earldom from the city of York, appears to have chosen Halton as the administrative centre for his land-holdings on both sides of the River Lune, which at low tide could be crossed on foot.

Over the years the country had become divided between members the Anglo-Saxon nobility with the most powerful families holding most of the land in the various earldoms. In the north however, with its strong Danish influence, the gathering of taxes had never been easy. Resentment smouldered under the surface and sedition was never far away. Tostig, although the son of a Danish princess, was regarded by Northumbrians as a representative of the Saxon line and never gained the respect and support that his Danish predecessor had enjoyed. In an attempt to gain firmer control he came down hard on those under his jurisdiction, particularly in the areas in which he held land in his own right.

Land-holdings then were measured in 'ploughlands', the amount of land that could be ploughed in a single day by one plough pulled by a team of eight oxen. One ploughland is estimated to have represented around 120 acres, said to have been the equivalent of the Anglo-Saxon 'hide' and the later Norman 'carucate'. When measured by the carucate (used in predominantly Danish areas) the amount of acreage appears to have varied county by county, area by area, depending upon the type and quality of the land and how much it could be expected to yield. Neither the hide nor the carucate, it seems, were actual measures of land, but simply units upon which taxation and other dues and commitments could be based.

The manor of Heysham, for example, when founded was assessed as three ploughlands, yet the total amount of land within its boundaries is estimated to have been 1,774 acres, far more than three times 120.

In Halton (according to the later *Domesday Book*) Earl Tostig had held six carucates, and the same in Slyne, Kellet and Lancaster. In Kirk Lancaster, Aldcliffe, Skerton, Newsham, Carnforth, Thurnham, Stapleton Terne, Hutton, Newton, Heaton, Oxcliffe, Torrisholme, Poulton and Bare, he held two carucates in each. In Bolton (le Sands), Overton, Middleton and Heysham - four carucates in each, and in Hillam one carucate.

Regarded by most of his vassals as cruel and repressive Tostig was deposed in 1065 while away hunting in the south with King

Edward. Two hundred major farm owners and their supporters rose against him and took York, the capital of his earldom, choosing Morcar (son of the Earl of East Anglia and grandson of Lady Godiva) to replace him as Earl of Northumbria. Soon, with an army reinforced by a contingent from Mercia (the earldom of his brother Edwin), the ambitious Morcar began to march south with a view to capturing the kingdom.

The powerful Earl Godwine had recently died leaving all Wessex (southern England from Land's End to Kent) to his son Harold, so King Edward ordered Harold to send an army against the insurgents. Instead Harold persuaded Edward to negotiate. As a result Morcar was officially recognized as Earl of Northumbria and Harold's brother Tostig was banished. He never forgave Harold, accusing him of supporting the uprising that had brought about his downfall. Presumably Morcar inherited Tostig's land holdings, including Heysham and the other villages attached to Halton, but this was never acknowledged by the later Normans.

--ooOoo--

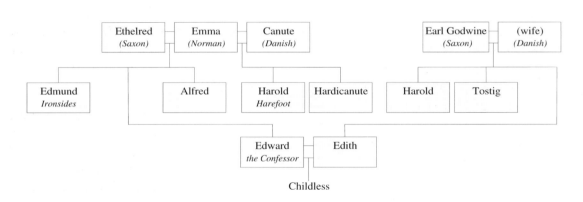

English aristocracy before the Norman invasion in 1066

13. The Norman Conquest

In January 1066 King Edward the Confessor died without leaving an heir. Harold was then elected King by a people who had grown weary of Edward's love of all things French and wanted nothing of the Duke of Normandy.

Within months Harold was fighting to defend his realm against his brother Tostig who had returned from exile in Norway. A pirate army shipped over from Norway by King Harold Hadrada had joined forces with Tostig and his supporters and taken the City of York. Brothers Morcar and Edwin, earls of Northumbria and Mercia, led an army against the invaders but were beaten and forced to retreat. Tostig and King Hadrada offered to make peace with the citizens of York provided they all marched south with them to conquer the realm, but then King Harold and his troops arrived. The two armies met at Stamfordbridge, and after a fierce battle in which both Earl Tostig and King Hadrada were killed the Norwegians surrendered. Of the 300 ships that had sailed from Norway, 24 were enough to carry back the survivors.

Harold then received news that William of Normandy had landed with an army of 7,000 men, announcing that he intended to take the throne of England promised to him by the late King Edward. After a hurried march south Harold's 5,000 exhausted and battle-weary troops faced William's superior force, fresh and newly-rested after an easy channel crossing.

The two armies met in battle on October 14th at Hastings in the Sussex countryside. King Harold was slain with two of his brothers and his army routed, although detachments of troops continued to fight on for several days until they were forced to surrender. William of Normandy had won his first battle on English soil, but more were to follow.

On Christmas Day 1066, after allowing his army to lay waste most of the southern counties (burning villages and slaying their inhabitants) William, Duke of Normandy, became William I of England. Soon afterwards rebellions broke out all over the country and attacks from marauding Danes were frequent. It took six more years before William could claim to be ruler of all England, but there were many who rejected this claim.

After stamping out all opposition King William re-established the 'County' or 'Shire' system, which had been introduced to some extent in non-Danish areas by the Anglo-Saxons. English landholders were dispossessed to be replaced by high-ranking Norman military men in return for a pledge of allegiance to the King and the promise to provide knights to serve in the King's army. The huge Anglo-Saxon land-holdings became subdivided into smaller, more manageable areas (or 'manors'), sometimes nothing more than a tiny hamlet and the land around it.

Anglo-Saxon rulers had earlier introduced and struggled to maintain a similar system with taxation and commitment to military service based on the 'hide' (the amount of land deemed necessary to support a peasant family), but the system had proved only moderately successful in certain areas. King William, however, imposed the Norman version with an iron fist. Soon the language of England became French and Latin, most English bishops and abbots were replaced by Normans, and English earls began to be replaced by Norman noblemen. The subjugation of the English proceeded relentlessly with nothing to halt the imposition of William's new system of administration until it spread too far northwards.

When the rebellious Northumbrians chose Morcar as their new earl they had sensed in him a kindred spirit. In 1071 Morcar and his brother Edwin led a rebellion against the new social order, reclaiming land that had been granted by King William to his Norman noblemen. In the north at that time the greatest of these Norman landholders was Count Roger de Poitou (third son of Roger of Montgomery) who was later to create the Manor of Heysham. The northern rebellion was short-lived, however, ending the same year with the death of Edwin and the routing of Morcar and his followers. Morcar escaped and fled to Ely where he joined his uncle, Hereward the Wake (second son of Earl Leofric and Lady Godiva), who had led an English uprising in 1070 and was still holding out against the Normans. Along with the bishop of Durham, who had also joined the uprising, Morcar was finally captured and imprisoned. Hereward evaded capture, but

is believed to have been murdered by the Normans shortly after being pardoned by King William.

After this William decided to deal decisively with the people of the ancient kingdom of Northumbria and to snuff out the flame of rebellion once-and-for-all. With his army he swept north burning and killing, destroying everything in his path, land, property and people alike. Very little escaped the pitiless ravages of his rampaging army. For example, of the 64 hamlets that had been attached to Preston, 48 were still uninhabited and the land unfit for cultivation at the time of the completion of the *Domesday Book* in 1086. A few people were said to have drifted back into some of the villages, but how many was not known. This had been one of the areas granted to Roger de Poitou before the Northumbrian rebellion, but now most of the Count's northern territories were regarded as worthless or unmanageable and had reverted back to the crown.

In addition to devastating the land King William's army had decimated the population leaving the whole of northern England with an average of less than three inhabitants to the square mile, many of them concentrated in the fertile areas around the rivers Lune and Wyre. In 1072, in an attempt to gain control of whatever there was of any value left in the north, William married off his niece Judith to the English Earl Waltheof of Huntingdon, who was then made Earl of Northumbria.

--ooOoo--

14. Count Roger de Poitou and the Manor of Heysham

William I died following a fall from a horse in 1087, shortly after the completion of the *Domesday Book*. On his death-bed he appointed his second son William heir to the throne. This resulted in a dispute over the crown between William and his older brother Robert.

Count Roger de Poitou appears to have supported William II in his struggle for the throne, and soon the Count's land in the north of England were returned to him with full powers to administer at his own discretion. In addition he was granted areas of land not previously held by him, including Heysham and the other settlements attached to Halton.

Throughout the rest of the country the huge Anglo-Saxon land holdings had already been broken up into more manageable areas of land, but until now this had not been attempted in the north, or if attempted had not been achieved.

Northumbria had been only loosely controlled at best by a succession of rebellious or (in the case of Aubrey de Coucy) incompetent earls, but Roger de Poitou was soon to change all that. As his centre of operations in the North West he chose the strategically situated village of Lancaster and began administering his affairs from within the walls of the ancient Roman Fort. With a private army of supporters at his command he soon established himself as lord and master, and then proceeded to dismember the vast estates once owned by Earl Tostig, reassessing their value and dividing them in the Norman tradition into small, individual manors.

A manor was usually equivalent to a holding which included a village with its own court and a hall, but this was not necessarily the case in troublesome Northumbria. As far as Roger de Poitou was concerned a manor was whatever he decreed it to be. The manors of Poulton, Torrisholme and Bare for example, with few inhabitants (possibly two or three families living in crude wooden huts), measured no more than a single ploughland each.

One thing was certain, Heysham, Poulton, Torrisholme, Bare, Heaton, Oxcliffe, Ovangle, Middleton, Overton and the rest, now all 'manors' in their own right, no longer 'belonged to Halton', they belonged to their creator, Count Roger de Poitou.

The term 'manor', from the Latin *manere* (to remain or to dwell), implies that the manor was the residence of the owner, held by him for the abode and use of his family (as opposed to 'tenemental land' which was granted out to under-tenants), but as most of the great land-barons held many manors and could not personally occupy all of them some were held in 'demesne' (managed on the landholder's behalf by a steward).

The term 'lordship' therefore applied only when land was managed by the lord himself (the tenant-in-chief or the under-tenant in the case of tenemental land) or by his family or someone in his immediate employ.

In 1093 Count Roger restored the ancient priory at Lancaster and commissioned the building of a small castle on the site of the old Roman fort. (No trace of this early castle exists today.) He then set about dealing with the affairs of his new estates.

Although there is no way of knowing how many of the newly-created manors Count Roger held personally at this time, Heysham appears to have been one of those retained by him until he disappeared from record. He granted 'one third' of the manor (Lower Heysham with its legendary religious structures and associations) to the Benedictine monks of St Mary's Priory in Lancaster, and the same year (1094) the prior granted St Peter's Church to the Abbey of St Martin of Sées, Normandy. From there it was passed to the Abbey of

Syon in Middlesex, but appears to have come once again under the jurisdiction of Lancaster Priory. The rector of St Peter's at the time is known to have paid a 'rent' of half a silver mark (6s 8d) per year to the prior, although how much land was involved is uncertain. Later priors continued to claim this fee from successive rectors until the 15th century.

The remainder of the manor included the hamlets of Upper Heysham, Over Heysham, Nether Heysham and Little Heysham, the entire holding having been reassessed as three ploughlands.

Count Roger then claimed the fishery rights along Heysham's foreshore by extending the boundaries of the manor seawards from the 'Merebeck' (the boundary stream which once flowed into the sea at Battery Point) to the mid-stream of the River Kent (which can be seen at low tide flowing the whole length of Morecambe Bay), along the Kent as far as the mid-stream of the Loyne. Then by various points to 'the ring edge of Middleton' and back to the Merebeck, 7,000 acres of foreshore encompassing all the mussel-beds in the area (with certain right granted to the Prior of Lancaster). From then on anyone fishing on the sands and mussel beds within those boundaries was obliged to pay 'mussel money' to the

St Peter's Church in 20th century

Lord of the Manor. These rights were not revoked until 1874 after a legal battle with local fishermen.

Since early times foreshore rights had belonged to the Crown. The terms of the charter agreed to by William II which granted these rights to the Manor of Heysham must have been uniquely binding, for the Duchy of Lancaster when founded was granted all foreshore rights along the entire coast of Lancashire, except those granted over three hundred years earlier to Count Roger de Poitou, and consequently to all succeeding lords of the Manor of Heysham.

One thing Count Roger had not foreseen was the early death of his friend and mentor, King William.

Because of his extravagant lifestyle and his treatment of the Church, William had become an unpopular King. He was killed by an arrow while hunting in the New Forest and it was suspected that he had been murdered.

In 1101, shortly after William's brother Henry had been elected King, Count Roger de Poitou lost his estates, for good this time, when they became once again the 'lands of the King'. Robert, elder brother of William and Henry, had been away on a Crusade when William was killed. On returning Robert claimed the crown but his army was defeated by Henry and he spent the rest of his life in prison. Count Roger is suspected of having supported Robert in his attempt to take the throne. This time he had backed the wrong horse!

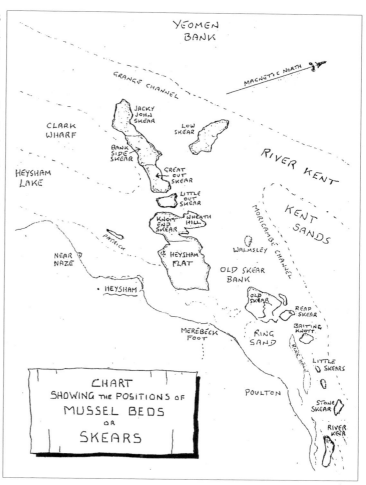

Sketch of a 19th century chart of the skears off-shore at Heysham and Poulton

--ooOoo--

15. The Lords of the Manor

Little is known about the Manor of Heysham for some time after this, although it is known that after Henry I had divested Roger de Poitou of his lands, Vivian Gernet (a relative of the Gernet family of Heysham) held the Manor of Halton in the King's name by 'knight service', the tenure under which the holder was obliged to perform 40 days general military service each year for the sovereign.

At Heysham one third of the manor was still held freely by the Prior of Lancaster, while the Gernet family appear to have held the remainder not by 'knight service' but by 'serjeanty', a tenure under which certain specific duties were stipulated.

There were two separate tenures whereby land could be held by 'serjeanty'. The first was 'Grand Serjeanty', by which the land was held on condition of rendering services to the King other than general military service, for example carrying the King's banner or lance when he went to war, or acting as the king's champion (challenging to single combat any who would deny the King's right to wear the crown), or serving the King as forester or carpenter, or in ways less known or less easy to define.

The second was 'Petit Serjeanty', by which the duties were often of a more servile nature, for example blowing a horn to warn of the coming of the King's enemies, or for any other purpose stipulated in the agreement. The commitment to horn-blowing continued for many years until the

duty was satisfied by payment of a rent. 'Petit Serjeanty' appears to have been the tenure by which the Gernet family held the Manor of Heysham.

It was during the reign of Henry II, in 1182, that Lancashire became a county. The lord of the Manor of Heysham at the time was Adam Gernet, known also as Adam of Heysham, while his son Benedict was lord of the Manor of Halton.

The county was soon divided into 'hundreds' (or 'wapentakes' in predominantly Danish areas), which were subdivisions of a county, each with its own assembly of notables and village representatives. The sheriff was the royal officer of the Shire, dealing with financial affairs and holding court for the entire county, while bailiffs presided at special sessions for individual hundreds. Both officers were responsible for dealing with felonies and crimes of violence.

When Richard (the Lionheart) became King in 1189 he granted the 'honour of Lancaster' to his brother, Count John of Mortain (now more popularly referred to as Prince John). The term 'honor' used in this context applied to a holding, or group of holdings forming a larger estate, of which the grantee now held overall lordship.

In 1194, Benedict Gernet, lord of the Manor of Halton (a major land owner and supporter of Count John) became rector of the Church of St Wilfred. At the time (and for many years afterwards) less-than-devout abbots, priors and rectors were able to amass their own private fortunes through the personal ownership of land and property, and the term 'rectory' (glebe house) came to apply to far more than just the building itself. The overall taxable value of 'the rectory' was based largely upon the financial returns from the glebe-lands and upon tithes which were appropriated from peasant farmers, fishermen and others, out of fear for their immortal souls.

During the 12th century the glebe-lands at Heysham covered over 50 acres (growing to 90 acres by the end of the 19th century) and successive priors of St Mary's and rectors of St Peter's are known to have acquired for themselves vast amounts of land and properties throughout the Manor of Heysham, of which the taxable value alone was staggering.

Brief accounts of legal matters such as the sale and purchase of the manor, disputes over land ownership and inheritance, and references to the births, marriages and deaths of the lords, ladies and landowners of the Manor of Heysham appear regularly in Manor Court documents over the next 300 years.

On a wider scale the most significant events to occur during this period include the signing of the Magna Carta, England's defeat by the Scots at Bannockburn, the rebellion of Thomas of Lancaster, the advent of the Black Death, the creation of the Dukedom of Lancaster, the Hundred Years War between England and France, the Peasant's revolt, the founding of the House of Lancaster, and the battles between the Lancastrians and the Yorkists popularly referred to as the Wars of the Roses.

Locally the most significant event was a raid on Heysham by the Scots in 1322.

After the rebellion of Thomas of Lancaster had led to a civil war in Lancashire between Thomas's supporters and those of the king, Scottish plunderers, in the absence of any organized resistance, began burning and pillaging their way through the county. On reaching Heysham the Scots were driven off by a quickly formed force of locals, but not before they had ravaged the area and destroyed many properties. Although the later Greese House was the first stone-built property known to have been occupied by Heysham's rectors, earlier rectories had existed since the 13th century. Records state that during the raid on Heysham by the Scots, the rectory of the day was partly destroyed, reducing its overall taxable value from £10 to £5. The term 'rectory' was obviously used here in its wider sense.

The affairs of Heysham began to take on a greater significance when, at an inquisition in 1501 held 'before the Feast of St George the Martyr' several men swore on the sacrament that Sir James Lawrence had died holding the manors of Heysham, Bolton (le Sands), Overton and Middleton. Lordship of the Manor of Heysham had apparently been acquired at some time in the past from the previous holders, the Harringtons.

Sir James' father, Robert Lawrence, had earlier married the daughter of Robert Washington, and through her had inherited the Manor of Carnforth.

After his father's death in 1450 Sir James is known to have held 'the Manor of Carnforth and other lands' by 'knight service', and also to have held the Manor of Middleton 'by the same tenure as that of the Manor of Heysham'.

When Sir James died in 1490 records state that he held the Manor of Heysham 'from the King as Duke of Lancaster' by 'socage' plus the rent (according to the legal terminology of the day) of 'one grain of pepper yearly'. Today the term 'peppercorn' applies in law to 'a very small rent'.

A dispute over lordship appears to have arisen in 1501 when the Stanleys, a renowned military family well favoured by the King, gained possession of the manor from Sir James' son, Lancelot Lawrence of Yealand, whose services to the King were non-military. Adding weight to the Stanley claim was undoubtedly the fact that Sir Edward Stanley had recently married Anne Harrington, daughter of Sir John, whose family had been the previous holders of the Manor.

Sir Edward Stanley (born c.1460) was to become the most notable Lord of the Manor of Heysham. Knighted during the reign of Edward IV he had acted as pall-bearer at the King's funeral. He was appointed sheriff of Lancashire by his stepbrother Henry VII in 1489, and became one of the King's personal knights. The same year he was granted lands and manors in Yorkshire, Lonsdale and Westmorland. Any dispute concerning lands or manors in which the Stanleys were involved was almost certain to be resolved in their favour. Edward's father, Sir Thomas, died in 1504, three years after the Stanleys had acquired lordship of the Manor of Heysham.

As an absentee lord and landowner much of Sir Edward's land was rented out, both at Heysham and throughout the rest of his vast estates, while the remainder was worked on his behalf by peasant farmers. Stewards or resident landowners appear to have administered the affairs of his numerous manors.

There is no way of accurately determining the layout of Heysham at this time. With ancient footpaths and cart tracks becoming modern roads it may be assumed that, before stone-built cottages replaced the earlier properties of the local inhabitants, Heysham village with its church, chapel and 'Royal Hotel' grain store, although more openly arranged, would have been little different than it is today. As for rest of Heysham, although all the original properties have long since disappeared, the de Moleynes are known to have had land and property along Old Middleton Road and to have owned the Water Mill where bows and arrows were manufactured. Apart from this single industry, however, Heysham was a purely agricultural area. At the time most of Heysham's mussel-gathering and fishing appears to have been carried out for the purpose of family consumption.

Agricultural practice since Anglo-Saxon times was based upon the open-field system, whereby the peasant's homes and farm buildings were clustered together in the centre of an area of arable land which was divided into three large 'fields', two in use with a third always laying fallow. Each field was divided into acre strips which were bought or rented by peasant farmers as they became available. In addition there would be an area of common pasture-land upon which cattle and sheep grazed, and an area of meadowland for the growing of hay. Beyond this was usually an area of waste land upon which landless or unemployed peasant families were allowed to build crude cottages. The system was partly communal as each man had to grow the same crop as his neighbour, although the produce was his own.

Exactly how Heysham's agricultural system operated is not clear. The area known as Lower Heysham included land on both sides of the village (a far more sizeable area before development than it appears today), and in addition there were four other areas (or hamlets) which existed within the boundaries of the Greater Manor. In relation to the village Nether Heysham appears to have been the most inaccessible, and here, as in some of Heysham's other (so far undeveloped) outer areas, the remains of old stone-built properties can be found. Heysham's oldest surviving property, however (with the obvious exception of St Peter's Church), is the main building of the

Royal Hotel, built around 1504 as a grain store.

After the Benedictine monks had vacated Lancaster Priory in 1414 the Rector of St Peter's came to be regarded as the 'lord' of Lower Heysham. With so much land owned by 'the Church' both here and in other parts of Heysham, the huge grain store was most likely built by the rector of the day, Philip Halstead and/or Sir Edward Stanley for the storing of their own produce.

Although the lord of the Greater Manor had no claim on Church land or its produce, an enquiry into the legality of Philip Halstead's institution, held at Heysham in 1488, found Sir Edward Stanley to be patron. Later, immediately after Sir Edward had acquired lordship of the manor, the grain store was built. Even as an Inn the property remained in the hands of the Church (or the local rector) until recent times.

When Henry VIII became king in 1509 he renewed the war with France and further angered the Scots who then invaded England, only to be defeated at the battle of Flodden in Northumberland on September 9th 1513.

At Flodden the Scots were under James IV, and the English were commanded by the Earl of Surrey. King Henry was away at Tournai engaged in battle against the French, so James IV of Scotland, who had declared himself to be an ally of the French, crossed the border with an invading army of 30,000 men. The English arrived, moved to the rear of the enemy, and launched a devastating attack with arrow and cannon. Both armies were grouped into four separate bodies, with the right wing of the English army commanded by Sir Edward Stanley, Lord of the Manor of Heysham. It was Stanley's Lonsdale archers who did the initial damage to the Scots, throwing them into confusion and forcing them to rush forward to fight at close quarters. For a while they appeared to be getting the better of the English, but with the help of Lord Dacre's reserve corps the English rallied. The Scots' right flank was completely routed when Sir Edward Stanley moved in with the troops under his command.

Then the Scots' left flank, led by James IV, attacked the Earl of Surrey and his men, but Stanley, turning his troops about, attacked James from the rear and succeeded in annihilating his entire corps. When the dust of battle had cleared the Scots had lost their King, about 10,000 men, and the best of all the Scottish nobility. The English had lost 5,000 men. Sir Edward Stanley, who had killed King James of Scotland by his own hand, was later mentioned in Sir Walter Scott's 'Marmion'.

The bows and arrows used against the Scottish forces to such devastating effect had been manufactured at Heysham, at the de Moleyne factory situated close to the site of the later Bobbin Mill (behind the present-day caravan park at the junction of Middleton Road and Trumacar Lane). Each arrow is said to have been marked 'The Grange', the name of the de Dacre residence at Higher Heysham. The bows were made from the finest yew, and the arrows from ash with specially hardened points. On November 23rd 1514, for valour in battle Sir Edward Stanley was made first Lord Mounteagle.

Manor Court documents recorded that in 1517 Lancelot Lawrence (who had lost the Manor of Heysham to Sir Edward Stanley) held land and property of Sir Edward Lord Mounteagle in Middleton by services not known. Later Lancelot Lawrence held land and properties of Lord Mounteagle in Heysham.

Sir Edward Stanley died in 1523 leaving a son, Thomas, who inherited the Manor of Heysham and succeeded to the title Lord Mounteagle. The title 'Earl of Derby' was retained separately by the descendants of George Stanley, Sir Edward's older brother. Sir Edward was buried at Hornby where he had created a religious foundation.

By this time the taxable value of Heysham Rectory was again estimated at £10, most of which was based on tithes. A few years later in 1535, although the Glebe House and lands were valued at only 20s, tithes were valued overall at £6 9s 8d. The old rent of 6s 8d now went to Syon Abbey.

In 1536 King Henry decided he wanted no more of the monasteries, and over the next three years their vast land-holdings and properties were confiscated, greatly enriching the King and his supporters. When Protestantism began to emerge the changes provoked several abortive rebellions, at one time involving several thousand active supporters from North Lancashire.

With Lancashire still remote and far removed from the direct control of central government the county was under the titular control of the powerful Stanley family (earls of Derby and lords Mounteagle) who provided Lancashire with a link to the throne, albeit a sometimes unwelcome one. Here the King's decrees proved difficult to impose and to police, as the Dissolution of the Monasteries had done little to weaken Lancashire Catholicism. Many people, landholders and peasants alike, continued to adhere to the old faith.

In 1553 Sir Thomas Stanley's son William (shortly before his aged father's death) attempted to mortgage the Manors of Ashton and Heysham to John and Thomas Brown. In regard to Heysham the transaction was disputed by other members of the family and the Manor was retained by the Stanleys.

During the reign of Mary Tudor Heysham disappears once again from the record books. In Lancashire generally the woollen industry was beginning to develop, although still mostly a cottage industry. The majority of woollen producers would work at home with the help of their families, selling their cloth to the best buyer. A large part of the woollen trade centred around the various Abbeys. Whalley Abbey alone took wool in tithes from eleven major chapelries. Heysham however, remained almost strictly agricultural, the main produce being oats, barley and beans, although there appears to have been some sheep farming and fishing, the latter still mainly for local or family consumption.

In 1577 Sir William Stanley lodged a complaint against certain people regarding peat cutting rights on Heysham Moss. It was customary to pay a few pence per year for the privilege. Also around 1577 Thomas Brockholes of Claughton, who held the Manor of Heaton from Sir Edward Stanley (Earl of Derby) and Sir Richard Houghton, had some disputes with Thomas Mashiter and others over entry to the moss and marsh lands at Heaton.

Several rights of way onto the moss lands still exist as public footpaths. One of them carries on from the end of Mossgate Road, through a passage-way between houses on the new estate, and across a bridge over the Harbour railway line. This joins a public footpath from Oxcliffe road which was presumably intended for peat-cutters from Poulton and beyond. These footpaths terminate at private pasture land, although a little-used public right-of-way continues from there across private fields, between farm buildings, and on to Mellishaw Lane. Access from Heysham to another part of the moss can be gained by following the public footpath past the site of the old Bobbin Mill.

In 1580 Sir William Stanley commissioned a survey of the Hornby estates, and referring to the Manor of Heysham the survey noted:

> My Lord hath within the Manor, Profits of Courts (fines etc), Felons' Goods (confiscated by the court), Wreck of the Sea, and other casualties as in the Rental Book called the Dimmission Book of 1530. Item, my Lord hath there Gressoms or Fines of the Tenants when the same doth happen, to wit, by the death of the Lord or Tenant and of either of them (as happened when Thomas of Heysham drowned himself on the Moss). Mussel Money paid by the Tenants of Heysham at the feast of Pentecost yearly, for which they are free to gather mussels from the Lord's lands, but these of late are annexed to the Tenants' rents.

Sir William Stanley died in 1581 leaving as his sole heir a daughter, Elizabeth, who was married to Edward Parker (10th Baron Morley). Edward, after spending some time abroad as a recusant, conformed, resigning the hereditary office of Lord of Ireland.

On Sir William Stanley's death his grandson, William Parker (son of Edward and Elizabeth), succeeded to the title Lord Mounteagle at the age of six in right of his mother.

In November 1583, Christopher Carus, William Wolfall and William Heysham (now a surname) purchased the Manor of Halton and various lands from Philip, Earl of Arundel. The following year they sold two barns in Heysham to Robert Bindloss, who was later said to hold land of the Queen 'as of her Manor of East Greenwich'. The tenure is said to have indicated that he held Church land. Also in 1583 Richard Shireburne purchased land in Heysham from Francis Turnbull and Thomas Bradley. (One John Bradley was later to purchase the Manor of Heysham.)

In addition to the de Moleynes' water mill, there was a wind-mill at Merebeck foot, the boundary between Heysham and Poulton. The last tenant died in 1584 without an heir so his brother, George Gibson, asked to become tenant. Sir William Stanley's survey of the manor had noted:

> The rent accustomed for both mills is 17s but the worth is £2 13s 4d per annum.

(The wind-mill survived until 1899.)

'T'Owd Mill' at Merebeck Foot
Etching by Roy Woodhouse (1897-1987)
(The Battery Inn is behind the cottages.)

Heysham Old Hall in early 20th century

By 1584 the construction of Heysham 'Old' Hall was well under way. It had been recorded earlier in the Stanley survey that Robert Edmondson held property containing 8 bays, 4 outbuildings and two gardens, with 14 acres of adjacent arable and meadow land, for which he paid 27s 4½d per annum. This, it has been asserted, can only have been Heysham 'Old' Hall. The survey of 1580 states:

> Note this tenement is divided into three parts whereof this Robert Edmondson hath half, his son William a fourth part and William Mashiter another fourth part: either fourth part is 9s 1½d rent with the mussel silver.

The Edmondsons who are known to have paid 'mussel money' at this time were Robert the elder, 3d; his son Robert, 1½d;

and William, 4d. Although parts of the building were still under construction it appears to have been advanced enough at the time of the survey of 1580 to accommodate its three tenants.

In accordance with his tenure Robert Edmondson, like most other smaller landholders, was obliged to work a number of days per year shearing sheep and ploughing the land belonging to the Manor House which was occupied at the time by John Clarkson the elder and his son, John Clarkson Jnr.

The location of the Manor House is difficult to determine. Since the time of the de Dacres none of the succeeding Lords of the Manor appear to have resided at Heysham. For their 29 acres of adjacent arable land the Clarksons paid an annual 'rent' of £4 13s 4d. It appears from this that the Clarksons may have been acting as stewards (holding the manor on the Parkers' behalf), in which case their residence, wherever it may have been, would have been regarded locally as the Manor House.

Along with the Mashiters the Clarksons are known to have been already well established at Heysham by 1543.

During the construction of Heysham 'Old' Hall a 'Priest Hole' was built into the rafters of the west wing with a passage leading from it between the inner walls to a well in the floor. This connected with a passage by the side of the chimney breast, and from there to an exit by a buttress around which outhouses were built. At the time the country was torn apart by deep religious divisions and the fanaticism of 'Bloody Mary' was still within living memory.

Because of Catholic plots to depose Elizabeth I, Mary, Queen of Scots was charged with treason and sentenced to death in 1587. Acting as commissioners at Mary's trial were Edward Parker, Lord of the Manor of Heysham, and Sir Henry Stanley (Earl of Derby), who had recently married Margaret Clifford, granddaughter of Mary Tudor.

Catholic monarchs across Europe were furious, and the following year the Spanish Armada attacked England.

In Heysham at the time Robert Baines of Whittington was holding land of William Parker (the young Lord Mounteagle) by 'knight service' and doing suit at the Court of the Manor. The duty of doing 'suit' (serving as an official at Manor Court hearings) dates from early Norman times when a 'freeman', with more land and therefore of higher rank than other peasants, was obliged to accept this duty in addition to his other commitments. Under other tenures the holder could be required to serve at the County Court.

In 1592, at the age of 17, William Parker married Elizabeth, daughter of Sir Thomas Tresham.

The following year William Mashiter appeared once again on record, this time as a tenant of Robert Dalton, an ancestor of the Daltons of Thurnham Hall. Although there is no indication at this point that the Mashiters held land of Lord Stanley, later Mashiters are known to have held and then owned for around four centuries the property known as Stanley Farm, an extensive holding situated between Old Middleton Road and Heysham foreshore.

In 1595 the Clarksons appear for the first time on record as landowners in their own right when Christopher and Thomas Clarkson purchased land and property in Heysham from Nicholas Johnson.

Two years later in 1597, William Parker sold the Manor of Heysham to John Bradley who died a few months after the purchase leaving the Manor to several co-heirs, and confusion inevitably followed.

--ooOoo--

16. Trouble in t' Manor

The construction of Heysham Old Hall was completed in 1598. A stone in the east gable bears this date, and beneath it is another stone twice inscribed with the initials 'R E' alongside a Tudor rose. Evidence indicates that William Edmondson was no longer in residence (possibly deceased), the building being then occupied as the initials suggest by Robert Edmondson the father, and his other son, Robert Jnr. (The Edmondson family continued to occupy the building until late in the 17th century.)

William Parker (who had recently sold the Manor of Heysham to John Bradley), although knighted by Queen Elizabeth in 1599, supported the Roman Catholic cause and became closely associated with the leading Catholic families. In 1601 he was involved in the Catholic rebellion in London with his father-in-law Sir Thomas Tresham and Robert Catesby, and as a consequence he was imprisoned for eight months in the Tower of London. He was released on payment of a massive fine.

Queen Elizabeth never married and produced no heirs, so before her death in 1603 she named James VI of Scotland, the Protestant son of Mary, Queen of Scots, as her heir. When James succeeded to the throne William Parker withdrew from his association with the Catholic extremists and appears to have relied upon the new king maintaining his allegedly tolerant attitude towards Roman Catholics. Later William wrote privately to James telling him of his desire to become a protestant, so James, who fought constantly with his parliament and welcomed any personal pledge of allegiance, rewarded William by summoning him to the House of Lords as Lord Mounteagle, a title which he had held previously only by courtesy in right of his mother Elizabeth.

Earlier in the year there had developed a Catholic plot to kill the Protestant king at the the opening of Parliament on November 5th, but now William wanted no part of it. He revealed the plot to Lord Salisbury and the arrest of Guido (Guy) Fawkes and his fellow conspirators followed. William Lord Mounteagle was regarded as the saviour of Parliament and was rewarded with land grants and a yearly pension.

After this William involved himself in colonial enterprises, becoming a member of the council of the Virginia Company and a shareholder in the East India and North-west Passage Companies.

In 1611 Jane, daughter and co-heir of the late John Bradley, married John Leyburne and is said to have carried the Manor of Heysham to the Leyburne family.

Heysham's oldest existing cottage appears to have been built around this time. This ancient stone-built property (bearing the initials I M) now stands adjacent to the rear of No. 4 Main Street, an early-19th century property known locally as the 'Manor

House'. The cottage had its own interior well, and the pump which once drew water from the well still exists.

A stone incorporated into the tiny extension in the north wall of St Peter's Church displays the same initials (I M) and a partly obliterated date which appears to read 1623. This stone and several accompanying date-stones can only have been transferred from demolished properties and re-used in the building of the extension.

In 1629 a row of stone-built cottages appeared at the entrance to Main Street in Heysham Village. Four years later a tiny extension with a date-stone bearing the initials E and C over T and C was added, creating the area known locally as 'Cosy Corner'. The empty space between these and the Royal Hotel cottages formed the entrance to Royal Fold, which was used for many years as an enclosure for sheep.

In 1631 Thomas Shireburne (son and heir of Richard), after declining knighthood was fined £10. One year later for recusancy in religion it was ruled that he should make an annual payment of £6 13s 4d. When Thomas died in 1635 he was said to have been holding the Manor of Heysham from the heirs of the late John Bradley, although Bradley's daughter Jane, who had married John Leyburne, was said to have passed to him 'lordship' of the Manor. Richard Shireburne, brother of Thomas, inherited the Shireburne estate.

In 1640, Charles I, who had clashed frequently with his parliament, marched into the House of Commons with an armed guard to arrest those members he regarded as the chief troublemakers. Shortly afterwards a civil war broke out and the country was once again divided in support of two opposing sides. The Royalists (Cavaliers) supported Charles, and the Roundheads (named because of their short hair cuts), led by Oliver Cromwell, supported Parliament. In Lancashire the towns in the south-east supported Parliament, while the country gentry on the whole were for the King. In 1642 the Royalists faced strong resistance from Manchester, and later, in 1644, the inhabitants of Bolton were massacred by the Royalist troops of the Earl of Derby.

In 1646 the whole of Lancashire was subject to Presbyterian organization which for a while replaced the Anglican church. Many dissenting sects began to arise and in a few years Furness and North Lancashire had become a centre of Quakerism. In North-West Lancashire, however, most people continued to cling determinedly to their old beliefs. This was the age of Edmund Robinson and his father, the notorious 'witch finders'.

The Royalists were finally defeated at Naseby and Charles surrendered to the Scots, but later was handed over to the English. In January 1649, after prolonged negotiation during which a second civil war broke out, Charles was executed. For the next 11 years, known as the Commonwealth period, England was a republic.

In 1650 the Manor of Middleton and its lands were purchased by William West, a colonel in Cromwell's army, and his wife Juliana.

At Heysham Richard Shireburne the younger, brother and heir of Thomas, had his estate sequestered for recusancy in religion. He died shortly afterwards in 1652.

Thomas Clarkson the younger, a Royalist, married Jane, widow of Richard Shireburne. Later Thomas had his estate sequestered by Parliament for having 'taken up arms against the state in both wars'. Jane had two thirds of her estate sequestered for 'recusancy only'.

At Bare William Leyburne forfeited his estate for being a Royalist.

Thomas Carus the elder forfeited his estates at Halton for 'popery and delinquency', and his son Thomas (Lord of the Manor of Halton) lost his estates for taking up arms against Parliament. He later regained them on payment of a fine of £467.

Thomas Brockholes (younger brother of John Brockholes, lord of the Manor of Heaton) was imprisoned in 1652 and his estates at Heaton forfeited and sold. Thomas admitted to having acted against the State at the beginning of the wars, but claimed that he had seen his error and subsequently did all he could in the parliamentary interest. His plea fell upon deaf ears.

The above estates were all confiscated by Parliament within three years of the appearance of Oliver Cromwell's Colonel William West.

West bought the property in Middleton now known as the 'Roof Tree Inn' (originally a farmhouse built by the monks of Cockersand Abbey), and in addition to his other lands and properties in Middleton he had land in Slyne and Hatlex (with fishery rights). Members of his family had land in Heaton and Overton, and in 1653 Richard Shireburne's estate at Heysham is said to have passed to Edmondson and West.

When Heysham Parish registers began in 1658 the very first page records the baptism of Jane, daughter of Richard Mashiter of the family of ancient yeomen, whose descendants went on to play an integral part in the political and social life of Heysham, eventually becoming Heysham's oldest surviving resident family. When Oliver Cromwell died the same year his son succeeded him as 'Protector' but was unable to keep control, and for years the country was in chaos.

Meanwhile the Edmondsons still occupied Heysham 'Old' Hall. Robert Edmondson (believed to have been the grandson of Robert the elder) married Jannette Clifton on November 13th 1659, and when their daughter Hellen was baptized on October 26th 1662, she was described as 'daughter of Robert Edmondson of the Hall'.

In 1665 came the Great Plague of London. This was followed a year later by the Great Fire. Greese House, the first stone-built Heysham rectory, appears to have been built around this time.

Greese House (or Cottage)

A stone bears the date 1680, while inside the building one of the main beams is inscribed with the initials F H and dated 1657. Either this beam came from an earlier demolished cottage, or the date stone marks a later extension. The property is said to have been built by John Clarkson, yet the rector of the day was William Ward whose family had been benefactors of Lancaster Priory and had managed the prior's affairs in lower Heysham since the 13th Century. The term 'Greese' is derived from the Latin word *gradus*, meaning 'steps', the main door being reached by a flight of seven steps.

Main Street developed a stage further in 1681 with the building of Yew Tree Cottage opposite St Patrick's Well.

24/26 Bailey Lane in the 1920s

In 1707 two adjoining cottages (numbers 24 and 26) were built in Quarry Road (now Bailey Lane). Number 24 was used for wool combing, the wool presumable having been sheered from sheep enclosed in Main Street's Royal Fold. A few meagre clues suggest that the Clarkson family (whose cottages stood on the edge of Royal Fold) were, among other things, the area's sheep farmers.

Around that time William Bushell, rector of St Peter's, built a new rectory in the church grounds to replace Greese House. A Latin inscription on the wall of the rectory stable states:

> By funds supplied by William Bushell's hand, I and the house for Heysham's rector stand.

(This rectory no longer exists.)

In 1715 the Jacobites rebelled in Scotland and the north of England in an abortive attempt to reinstate a Catholic king. The term 'Jacobite' derives from the Latin *Jacobus* (James) after James II of England, and is the name that was given to the followers of the Stuart house, although the later Stuarts received their main support from the Scots.

After the Jacobites had surrendered at Preston the Manors of Heysham and Nateby were forfeited by the Catholic Leyburnes for their involvement in the rebellion. The Manors were then sold to Croft Coles of Holborne, marking the end of an era, at least as far as Heysham was concerned.

--ooOoo--

South end of 26 Bailey Lane in 2000
The original mullion windows can be seen in the left gable.
The other gable is a recent addition incorporating an old window
found in the west wall

17. Twilight of the Manor

At Heysham in 1723/1724 the bells of St Peter's Church were installed. Each bell was inscribed with both dates and with the names Edmund Edmundson and John Chaffer, who are believed to have been the churchwardens.

Around this time, on July 24th 1724, Parliament (in the name of King George I) granted licence to

Gate House to Heysham Lodge

the Mayor, Bailiffs and Commonalty of Lancaster to hold in mortmain the Manor of Heysham with all customs and rights for the sum of £470.

On the death of William Bushell in 1735, Thomas Clarkson (vicar of Chipping), son of William Clarkson of Heysham, became rector of St Peter's. The Clarksons had been one of Heysham's leading families since the mid-16th century, until the family's estates were forfeited to Oliver Cromwell's Parliament. (The Christian name Thomas appears to have been a Clarkson favourite. There were three later Thomas Clarksons, all Rectors of St Peter's Church, in 1756, 1796, and 1819.)

Apart from the occasional payment of 'mussel money' to the Corporation of Lancaster nothing more is heard of The Manor of Heysham until it appeared on record again in 1766 when the manorial rights were sold for £672 to a group of Heysham freeholders.

The land later to become Heysham Head was bought by George Wright who presumably built The Lodge, now more popularly referred to as the Gate House, at the entrance to his property just off Barrows Lane. The exact date of the building of Heysham Lodge, the Great House on Heysham Head, originally named 'The Barrows', is uncertain.

In some areas new agricultural practices were being introduced. Gentleman farmer Lord 'Turnip' Townsend and other rich landowners were attempting to convince farmers in general of the benefits of planting turnips and other root crops. These would clean and revive the soil, ending the need for wasteful fallow, and would provide excellent food for cattle. Meanwhile another gentleman farmer, Jethro Tull, had introduced a more scientific method of sowing, and had invented the first seed-planting drill.

Small farmers, however, resisted these changes. Whereas the richer landowner could afford to enclose his land and risk experimenting with these new techniques, the small farmer could not. The decision by the group of Heysham freeholders to purchase the manorial rights from Lancaster Corporation meant that with no Lord of the Manor or major landholder to contend with, they could resist as a body for as long as possible any attempt to impose these new practices upon them.

Heysham was silent again during this period until, in December 1802, a complaint was made by Richard Bagot against Christopher Orr respecting the right to

> certain places or closes on the shore near Heysham called The Foot Mussel Skear and The Great Out Mussel Skear.

The complaint was upheld and the disputed areas were declared to belong exclusively to the plaintiff

> as Trustee for the Lords of the Manor of Heysham.

Two years later an entry in the Manorial Books noted:

> ... received from the Rev Mr Clarkson for one year's rent of the 'Out Skears', three pounds three shillings, and received from William Hadwen for permission to fish within the boundaries of Heysham, one shilling.

From the late 17th century, when the Edmondsons finally vacated Heysham 'Old' Hall, little is known about its owners or occupiers until 1805, when the premises were occupied for two years by Samuel Bailey of the 9th Regiment of the Light Dragoons, and then for three or four years

by Richard Caton who purchased the property on June 1st 1807. Both of these gentlemen owned large amounts of land and properties in other parts of Heysham. (Quarry Road later became Bailey Lane.)

In 1810 Heysham House (now Penhale Court) was built by the Tatham family. Again little is known about the occupants of this typical Georgian house. A Preston M.P., Sir William Tomlinson Bart, lived there for some time, and more recently did Councillor R C Penhale (President of the Old Folk's Movement) after whom the property is now named. The last owner, Alderman William Curwen, gave the house and grounds to the local council to be used as an Old Folk's Home, or (in the language of the more politically correct) a Senior Citizen's Retirement Home.

One Thomas Caton died on January 3rd 1811, and the same year, on November 30th, Heysham Old Hall and lands adjacent were sold by auction by Richard Caton. In the past this dwelling has been sometimes mistakenly referred to as the 'Manor House', although none of its owners or occupiers were ever lords, or even stewards, of the Manor of Heysham. A poster once preserved at the Hall gives particulars of the property of Richard Caton due to be sold by auction at The Royal Oak in Lancaster. Here the building is referred to as the 'Mansion House', or Heysham Hall, commonly called 'Wren Hall'. (The second Heysham Hall was built several years later, giving cause for the inclusion of the term 'old' in reference to the first.)

--ooOoo--

18. Heysham: The Negative and the Positive

In 1820 Dr Thomas Dunham Whitaker, well-known antiquarian and Rector of St Peter's (1813-1819), wrote about Heysham:

> Of this parish it is remarkable that there is no market, no shop, and until last year no butcher, no medical practitioner, no attorney, no endowed school, no sea boat, and thanks to the want of water no manufactory ... In the whole parish there is not a spring of clear and tasteless water, the wells being mere puddles, and those too rendered brackish by some secret communication with the sea through crevices in the rocks. Two or three gentlemen's families reside here, to the great advantage of the poor, for the salubrity of the air. The rest of the population is divided between a race of old yeomanry, tenants at rack rents, and poor families earning a wretched subsistence by unskilful fishing.

Heysham at that time (as recorded by Baines in 1825) was

> a place of fashionable resort for sea-bathing,

but the visitors were

> more select than numerous.

This record contains information derived from the 1801 census followed by names, dates, facts and figures extending over a 25 year period. Baines states that there were 110 dwellings occupied by 106 families (a total of 540 persons), and 93 of these families were employed in agriculture. Of the others nine were in trade and four 'in professional pursuit or unemployed'. At the conclusion of the record is a 'Directory'.

Listed in the Directory as residing in 'Heysham Parish, Higher Heysham' are the following:-

Henry Bains	Dobson's Hotel
Mrs Jane Banks	
Joseph Burrows	Parish Clerk
Thomas Cowell	Yeoman
John Foxcroft	School Master
Mrs Hadwin	
Miss Mary Hadwin	Lodger
John Dodgson	Yeoman
John Mashiter	Yeoman
John Mashiter Jnr	Yeoman
Rev Roger Mashiter	
John Menzies Esq	
James Proctor	Bathing Machine Man
Rev Thomas Yates Ridley MA	
Thomas Wilkinson	Lodger Morecambe Cottage
John Worthington	Lodger Morecambe Cottage
George Wright	The Barrows

The term 'Heysham Parish' referred to the whole of Heysham while 'Higher Heysham' referred to the area around Middleton Road where Heysham's leading citizens and biggest landowners lived, although some of the above individuals appear to have been erroneously placed.

Both Dr Whitaker and the compiler of the 'Directory' failed to mention that amongst Heysham's 'race of old yeomanry' were the current holders of the manorial rights, and just how many Heysham residents 'earned a wretched subsistence by unskilled fishing' is open to question.

In 1797 Joseph Mallard William Turner, one of the greatest of British artists, had first visited the area after crossing Morecambe sands by coach from Ulverston. He was so impressed with the breath-taking views across Morecambe Bay that he returned in 1816. On the 8th of August he visited Heysham where he made several sketches from which he later produced such works as *Heysham and Cumberland Mountains*. The vantage point for the latter appears to have been the high ground at the seaward end of present day Woborrow Road, before development blocked the view.

At the time Heysham was experiencing 'the constant influx of opulent and well-dressed people' who were attracted to the place by 'the superiority of the accommodations'. Turner is said to have spent a night at Greese Cottage (although this observation may give rise to some contention) and being a man who enjoyed a pint or two of ale it seems certain that he would have found time to sample the local brew at Dobson's Hotel.

A reclusive and secretive man, Turner most likely quaffed his ale silently and alone, speaking to no-one about himself or his work. He was already a successful artist and a Professor of the Royal Academy School of Art, yet no local tales of his visit

to Heysham have ever emerged to become embellished with the passing of time.

The great artist, born on April 23rd 1775, in Maiden Lane, Covent Garden, passed away peacefully in Chelsea on December 19th 1851, leaving to the nation nearly 20,000 works of art.

Tower Cottages in the late 20th century

Around the time of Turner's visits to Heysham, Heysham Tower was built by J T Knowlys Esq (the exact date is not known). Intended as a gentleman's residence the premises stood in thirteen acres of private land surrounded by a high wall. Soon it became the annual meeting place of 'John o'Gaunt's Bowmen'. At an archery competition on September 30th 1831, the first prize was won by none other than J T Knowlys Esq.

Platforms in the Rectory Wood
The stone staircase may be much older.

After visiting the scene of Turner's *Heysham and Cumberland Mountains* (c.1830) John Ruskin wrote in his work on 'Modern Painters':

> The subject is a simple north-country village on the shores of Morecambe Bay; a single street of thatched and chiefly clay-built cottages, the roofs so green with moss that at first we hardly discern the houses from the fields and trees ... Beyond the village is a rocky hill, deep set with brushwood, a square crag or two of limestone emerging here and there, with pleasant turf on their brows, heaved in russet and mossy mounds against the sky ...

Ten years earlier, around 1820, Dr Dunham Whitaker had written:

> Above the rectory begins a line of perpendicular rock, which shelters both that and the village at once from the sun and the storms; but notwithstanding this partial disadvantage, fruit trees and garden vegetables are seen to thrive on platforms won out of the rock.

In less than ten years, it seems, the fruit and vegetables had been replaced by brushwood. The 'platforms', shored up by walls of stone, are still in evidence today, but judging by the above descriptions the wood that now covers this ancient ceremonial area is of comparatively recent origin.

By 1836 the Manor of Heysham had become divided into sixteen shares which were held by 12 freeholders who appear to have been so far successful in resisting the practices being enforced in most other parts of the country. Although a freeholder, unlike tenant farmers and others, could not be driven off his land he had to pay towards the substantial cost of any neighbouring enclosures, or sell the land. The 'Open-Field Enclosure Act' was officially passed on December 3rd 1836.

On the very same day the Saturday Magazine (published under the direction of The Committee of General Literature and Education) described Heysham Village as seen from Turner's *Heysham and Cumberland Mountains* vantage-point.

Heysham and Cumberland Mountains : J M W Turner
© Copyright   The British Museum

A prettier composition of scenery of a simple and placid character I have seldom seen. The cottages are disposed without any formality at various elevations on the side of a steep bank, with small gardens and orchards amongst them, and honeysuckles creeping around the doors and casements ...

The writer then went on to observe:

It would appear from the remains of tombs which are still in existence in the churchyard, that the little village of Heysham was once a place of greater note than it is at present. Many tombstones and fragments of them are scattered about the churchyard, which, from the symbols and ornaments upon them, are evidently of no modern date. A sword and a cross are the more frequent symbols by which they are distinguished, but I (noticed) upon one a sword and a harp.

--ooOoo--

19. Wrights, Royds & Railways

The second Heysham Hall was built in 1839 by Thomas Rawesthorne and his wife, Ann. At the time one Thomas Rawesthorne was the owner of Heysham 'Old' Hall, and although apparently the same person there is no existing evidence to substantiate this. The headstone on the family grave in the grounds of St Peter's Church refers to him as 'Thomas Rawesthorne of Heysham Hall'. A stone at Heysham Tower inscribed with the date 1839 and the initials R over T and A is known to have come from Heysham Hall while it was later being partly demolished. The Thomas Rawesthorne of Heysham Hall was a solicitor practising in Lancaster in partnership with a Mr R Lawrence.

Both Heysham Tower and Heysham Hall are believed to have been built on the sites of dwellings of great antiquity, The Hall on the site of 'The Grange', home of the de Moleyne family of Heysham, and Heysham Tower on the site of the Dacre residence.

In 1846 Heysham 'Old' Hall was mortgaged by Thomas Rawesthorne to John Fearnside and John Brockbank, two directors of the Lancaster Banking Company. John Brockbank died the following year and John Fearnside three years later, and the interests of the Lancaster Banking Company passed to Edmund and Elizabeth Fearnside (John's widow). The very next day the Lancaster Banking Company made a valuation of Heysham Old Hall, 'the property of T Rawesthorne Esquire'.

In 1848 the North-Western railway came to Poulton (already a popular sea-bathing resort), and the following year the first excursion trains from Leeds and Bradford arrived.

Two years later in October 1850 Mr J T Knowlys of Heysham Tower died from the effects of a pistol shot, the circumstances of which are not known.

Thomas Rawesthorne of Heysham Hall died on November 27th 1854, leaving ten children. His two eldest daughters opened a school in the first two houses (now numbered 310 and 311) to be built in the area that was later to become Eidsforth Terrace, situated at the far end of Morecambe Terrace at the seaward end of Lord Street. One of these ladies, believed to be Mary J Rawesthorne, retired and went to live in Lincolnshire with her friend Mrs Marsden, wife of the late Rev Maurice Howard Marsden, Rector of Poulton.

The 'Great House' on Heysham Head passed to an army surgeon, Captain George Wright, who had returned from the Crimean campaign in 1855. This George Wright was the grandson of George Wright the previous occupier, who had been steward to John Marsden at Wennington Hall and Hornby Castle. The new owner changed the name from 'The Barrows' to 'The Lodge' and for a while enjoyed the quiet, idyllic life of a country gentleman. Later tragedy struck when his two daughters, Harriett and Mabel, were drowned while swimming at

Half Moon Bay. Their graves can be found in the grounds of St Peter's Church directly below St Patrick's Chapel.

In March 1857, Elizabeth and Edmund Fearnside transferred their rights to Heysham Old Hall estate to William Jackson of Lancaster and Joseph Bushel of Myerscough who, on October 17th the same year, conveyed the property to John Royds, Rector of St Peter's Church since 1858. (Joseph Bushel was possibly a descendant of William Bushell who had been Rector in 1698.)

While St Peter's Church was being restored and extended by John Royds in 1864 the ancient Anglian doorway was discovered and rebuilt stone by stone in the Church grounds. At the time John appears to have been employing No. 4 Main Street (the 'Manor House') as a temporary rectory.

On the death of John Royds in 1865 (according to date-stones on the outside wall of the east wing) ownership of Heysham Old Hall passed first to Rev Charles Smith Royds (Rector of Houghton) until his death in 1879, and then to his son Charles Twemlow Royds, who had been Rector of St Peter's since the death of John. While continuing to use the 'Manor House' as a rectory Charles Twemlow set about restoring Heysham Old Hall which had fallen into disrepair after being used for some time as a farm house. It was during this restoration work that the 'priest hole' was discovered.

In 1874 a Poulton fisherman, Robert Fawcett, took mussels from the Heysham skears without obtaining permission from the Lords of the Manor and court action followed. Mr Russel, Q C for the defence, claimed that Heysham foreshore and its mussel beds belonged to the Duchy of Lancaster. Surprisingly this was not challenged and the claim was sustained, the jury finding in favour of the defendant. As a consequence the Lords of the Manor of Heysham later abandoned their claim to exclusive rights of fishery.

In 1885 Poulton (le Sands) became Morecambe. It is believed that the term 'Moricambe' was used originally by Ptolemy in reference to the bay as being the estuary of the rivers Lune and Kent. The old local name for the bay was 'Kent Sands', or simply 'The Sands'.

Nothing more is heard of the Manor of Heysham until 1897 when, with a view to enhancing the prosperity of Heysham, Mr William Tilly of Morecambe, steward of the Manor since 1880, sold on behalf of the proprietors 'considerable portions' of Heysham foreshore to the Midland Railway Company for the construction of the new harbour. The proprietors at the time were

Miss Harriet Caton
Francis Frederick Grafton
J F T Royds
F W Smalley
George Wright
Miss Anne Thompson
the Knowlys trustees
the representatives of the late Col Marton
Thomas Mashiter
John George Wright

A large part of the land sold to the Midland Railway Company was owned at the time by Robert Henry Mashiter of Stanley Farm, who was also a churchwarden and a member of the Heysham Parish Council.

Contractors for the Midland Railway Company, Messrs Price and Mills, began work on the harbour the same year. The two thousand men (some with wives and families) who were employed on its construction were housed in 'villages' on the site, and, because the commencement of the work coincided with the Gold Rush, the two villages were named appropriately Klondyke and Dawson City.

Each village had its own shops, canteen, post office, school, recreational facilities, chemist, surgery, and even an isolation hospital. Nothing, not even an outbreak of smallpox, would be allowed to interrupt the work once in progress.

Heysham Hall had been occupied by the Grafton family, and Heysham Tower by the Cawthras, until the building of the harbour began, then both properties were used by the railway authorities as temporary hotels.

In 1898, as a result of the massive increase in population, the law came to Heysham with the building of the Knowlys Road Police Station.

--ooOoo--

Shops in the Klondyke Village at Heysham Harbour

20. Decline and Fall

In 1899 the old mill at Merebeck Foot was demolished. Since the death of the last tenant, Betty Hudson, the mill had been used as an arms and ammunition store by the 24th Lancashire Artillery Volunteers who engaged in gunnery practice by firing their cannons out towards the open sea.

Also in 1899 the Heysham parish council was replaced by an urban district council consisting of twelve members under the chairmanship of the Rev Charles Twemlow Royds. Prominent amongst the council members were Mr Robert Henry Mashiter, who had served previously on the Heysham Parish Council since its formation, and Mr Thomas Mashiter, an extensive land owner and one of the proprietors of Heysham Manor. (Thomas Mashiter remained a member of the urban district council for fourteen years.)

Heysham's new harbour was officially opened on September 1st 1904, with the sailing of the SS Antrim captained by William Hill (who became Marine Superintendent and later Harbour Master). There had been a trial run the previous month, when Captain Dunlop had taken the SS Londonderry to the Isle of Man and back carrying 900 passengers on a day excursion.

The Victoria History, published shortly after the turn of the century, describes Heysham thus:

> Lower Heysham, in spite of the many recent changes, remains a picturesque village with many quaint houses. In recent times the healthiness of the place has attracted summer visitors, so that even in 1826 Heysham was a fashionable resort for sea bathing. The ancient churches are visited by great numbers of those who spend their summer holidays in Morecambe and its neighbourhood. The establishment of the railway harbour may lead to other commercial enterprises.

A crest designed for Heysham
(after Harbour construction)

Apart from providing some work over the years however, Heysham in general was never to benefit from the existence of the new harbour. Boat trains from the cities carried passengers straight to the docks, bypassing Heysham completely.

In 1909 the Medical Officer of Health at Heysham reported that many houses in Lower Heysham had been provided with water closets in place of earth closets and a good many had also been supplied with the town's water. For the past 200 years the major source of water had been the village

Village Pump
(accidentally destroyed in 1930)

pump at the junction of Bailey Lane, Knowlys Road and St Mary's Road, although in the past the other wells mentioned by Dr Whitaker, St Patrick's Well in Main Street and St Mary's Well a few yards up the hill above the village pump, had provided some drinkable water. These two wells still exist. St Patrick's (now dry) can be found beside the road at the turn-off to St Peter's Church, and St Mary's (previously known as 'The Sainty Well') in the garden of a private house in St Mary's Road. Also in 1909 the wooden huts at Dawson City, which were an eyesore and a source of danger in the event of a fire or an outbreak of infectious disease, were finally closed.

On August 4th 1914 Britain entered the First World War. A coalition Government was formed the following year, and at Heysham the rectory was speedily converted into an auxiliary hospital for wounded soldiers. The rector at the time was Charles Cradock Twemlow Royds.

According to the 1917 Christmas edition of Heysham's *Hospital Gazette and Calendar* the hospital opened in the Spring of 1915 with 10 beds, which soon increased to 15 at the request of the authorities. Dr Herd provided the necessary medical attention 'with skill and unfailing kindness', while a regular nursing staff took care of the patients' general welfare. Assisting the regular staff were many local people who offered their services voluntarily, resulting in the patients being outnumbered by those who were attending to their needs. Soldiers who were able would lend a hand inside the hospital or around the grounds, gathering fruit or tending to the rectory ponies, while some would go off on shopping expeditions or run errands in 'the big trap' drawn by Tommy the horse. On 'Doctor's mornings' though, heaven help the man who forgot that

> patients must content themselves in the grounds, or within hearing of the big bell which, from its turret on the roof, can be heard all over the lower village.

In 1916 the Conscription Bill was passed, Lloyd George became Prime Minister, and wounded soldiers continued to pass through the caring hands of the staff at the Heysham

Rectory Auxiliary Hospital with such ceaseless regularity that an anonymous local poet was moved to pen the lines

> Many have fought for us, many have
> bled for us,
> Many their lives have given.
> Shall we not therefore do our best
> For those who have nobly striven?

And the 'best' they certainly did! Croquet tournaments and bowling competitions were arranged, and garden parties at which visiting minstrel troupes would perform, or at which open-air plays would be staged. A Mr Giddings undertook all dispensing free of charge, and Mr Jenkinson arranged regular outings for the patients either in horse-drawn carriages or in motor cars borrowed from other Heysham residents. During the winter months there were whist drives, billiards handicaps and concerts, the latter often being staged by the soldiers themselves before audiences of local people.

The war ended in November 1918, and a Memorial bearing the names of the men of Heysham Village who died in the fighting can be found in the grounds of St Peter's Church.

In the grounds of the Strawberry Gardens Hotel at this time were aviaries, greenhouses, conservatories, and of course, strawberry gardens, where for a penny visitors could pick their own strawberries. In 1920 the original owners, the Wyton family, sold the property to a development company and soon these attractions had disappeared to make room for houses and shops. Only the hotel and car park remained. The hotel was later sold to Mr Walter Birtles of the Crown Hotel, Morecambe.

A description of Heysham around 1920 follows on the next two pages. This description, written many years later by Mr F Dodgson, is presented verbatim by kind permission of his daughter, Mrs Beatrice Tollitt, of Bailey Lane.

Strawberry Gardens Hotel in the late 20th century
(from Knowlys Road)

Heysham around 1920 as remembered by Frank Dodgson
(with editorial notes in italics in brackets)

Where the little park is at Heysham bus terminus was a little farmhouse, and the next buildings on that side of Heysham Road were the two houses which are nearly opposite Longlands Lane. The next building on that side was a farmhouse at Four Lane Ends where the grocery store is now. There were no other buildings on the Heysham side of Cross Cop.

On the other side of the road was the Old Hall Inn (then a private house), then the Old Hall farm buildings (where St James Church & Hall now stand), and the house which was used as the farmhouse. The next buildings were the library (then the council office), then the Police Station.

The other side of Knowlys Road was the Strawberry Gardens and the range of buildings belonging to the Strawberry Gardens which was a sort of pleasure ground, with swings etc., for children and a lot of glass houses with all kinds of plants in them. Heysham Avenue was there but not fully built up, and the next buildings were Royds Avenue which is just before the Cross Cop Hill.

The Morecambe side of Cross Cop has not greatly altered as long as I can remember.

Knowlys Road started at the Police Station and ended at No. 26, and then it was fields as far as the two old houses at the end of Eardley Road, and

to get to Heysham Road from that point one had to go up the little lane which is still there but is now overgrown. One side of Eardley Road was there but between those houses and Woborrow Road was a triangular shaped field known to us boys as Dickies field but I do not think that was its proper name. St Patrick's Walk was not yet built and was just green fields.

Going out of the village up Heysham Hill (*Crimewell Lane*) the right hand side was as it is now, except a house and Smithy which were tacked on to what is now the first house (*Holly Bank*). On the other side was the red brick building which is now flats and only two more houses just past Longlands Avenue. Longlands Avenue was of course not there at that time.

In the village the present Chinese Café was the Cooperative Society grocers shop until 1923 when the Cooperative Society demolished a barn and stable and built a new shop with a house attached. The Cooperative shop is now a kind of shoe shop and what was the house has just opened as a café (*now Curiosity Corner*).

Further up the Main Street on the left was the Royal Fold, with I think, five cottages (two still standing but not in use) and some farm buildings. That area is now the Royal Hotel car park. The shop opposite the entrance to that car park was a cow shippon as also was the building opposite the Hotel. Where the newish house (*probably Barrows House*) near the Church gate is, was also a barn and shippon. At that time Heysham still had a good lot of farms and I append a list of their names starting from the Middleton end:

Broadgate Foot	Mr H Steel
Long Whitley	Timothy Barton
Trumacar (House still there)	Robert Burrow
Banks House	Anthony Hilton
Stanley	Mrs Mary Mashiter (My Granny)
Town End	John Mashiter
Central (Now D.I.Y. shop)	John Clarke
Old Hall	Rich Crayston
Four Lane Ends	Thomas Wilcock
Winterend	John Willacy
Blackberry Hall (Still standing)	Thomas Procter
Fanny House (1)	Thomas Outhwaite
Fanny House (2)	Edward Gorst
Whitham House	Thomas Pearson
Lordsome	Mr Newsham
Lordsome Hill	Charles Grey
Crow Dubs	Mr Newsham

Most of these farmhouses are now demolished except the two Fanny Houses, both now farmed by James Birkett, and Whitham House still farmed by the Pearson family. There was also a little farm in the village called Salem Farm and the house is at the entrance to the Cliff path and still occupied by the grand-daughter of Robert Swindlehurst who was the farmer at the time I am writing about.

Most of the land is still used for the grazing of cattle.

Heysham Road was not very wide and not very straight and had a tram track running from the Battery to the Strawberry Gardens. The trams at that time were petrol driven and during the 1914-18 war, owing to the shortage of petrol, they were driven by gas and had huge canvas gas holders on top.

I think it would be about 1924 or thereabouts when a Mr Jenkinson bought an old London bus and started a service from the Battery to the village. This of course took the trade from the trams and so the Heysham Tramway Company in turn bought a secondhand bus from somewhere. This bus was bright yellow and was soon christened 'the biscuit tin'. There was great rivalry between these bus operators for a time, but soon a bigger firm called County Motors joined in and they travelled further afield, at least to Lancaster.

Little is known of the history of Heysham's Royal Hotel since its initial use as a grain store in the 16th century, although it appears to have been converted first into a dwelling during the late 17th/early 18th century, and later, towards the end of the 18th century, into a 'public house'. In February 1922 the property was conveyed jointly to the Reverend Charles Craddock Twemlow Royds, Messrs A and J F Barker (brewers of Lancaster), and Mr J Pullan. The tenant at the time was Mr John Pearson who was also a farmer.

Heysham Hall was bought three months later (in May 1922) by Mr Goulden of the Grafton Hotel, Morecambe, although whatever plans he may originally have had for the property are not known. (The Grafton, situated at the corner of Skipton Street, later became the Savoy.)

In March 1924 the Royal Hotel was re-conveyed to the Reverend Royds; the Barkers; and J Pullan (possible on the death of Mr Pearson whose wife took over the tenancy until her retirement), and just 19 days later it was conveyed jointly once again to J Pullan, the Barkers, and the Lancaster and District Cooperative Society Ltd. Later it passed to the Executors of William Mitchell.

In 1925 Heysham Tower became Morecambe Bay Holiday Camp run by Mr and Mrs B S Holden. Later the camp was able to accommodate 400 in the main house and another 100 (men only) in tents in the grounds. A strict set of rules and regulations were enforced, ensuring that a good time was had by all.

In 1926 the area known as Heysham Head was bought by Septimus Wray of Ilkley who turned it into an Amusement Park with band arena, zoo, rose garden (later to feature children's 'talent competitions'), open-air dancing, swings, rides, and an open-air theatre. 'The Great House' (Heysham Lodge) became part café, part residence, and later an amusement arcade containing several mechanically operated devices that were ancient even then, and would by now have been priceless.

Two years later, in 1928, it was felt that the interests of Heysham would be better served through the offices of Morecambe Corporation. An amalgamation was arranged and the official ceremony took place on October 1st at the old district boundary in front of the Battery Hotel. One year later Heysham foreshore from the Battery to Half Moon Bay was sold to Morecambe Corporation by the Lords of the Manor for £800.

On July 15th 1930 the village pump at Heysham was destroyed by a motor vehicle and the wreckage taken away by Morecambe Corporation.

Heysham Hall was partly demolished in 1933 and turned into flats by Alan Robinson and Sons on behalf of Mr Shackleton, who used stonework from the Hall to build a row of cottages in Smithy Lane.

Two years later, in 1935, Roger de Poitou could be heard turning in his grave when the mussel industry suffered a blow from which it never really recovered. Mussels from Morecambe Bay were declared unfit for human consumption because of sewage contamination.

When Septimus Wray died in 1936 the Amusement Park on Heysham Head, after being divided into 10 shares, continued to be managed by his son, Fred.

As the international situation rapidly deteriorated war seemed inevitable, but Britain's rearmament was slow and apathetic, the governments of Prime Minister Baldwin and then Neville Chamberlain adhering to a near-fatal policy of appeasement. On September 3rd 1939, however, as a consequence of Germany's invasion of Poland, Britain went to war. Under the National Service Bill all men aged between 18 to 41 were made liable to be called upon for military service. The following year Winston Churchill replaced Neville Chamberlain as Prime Minister.

As a defence against the landing of enemy craft the entire length of Morecambe Bay sands bristled with huge wooden posts, the holiday camp at Heysham Tower was quickly converted into a training camp for officer cadets, concrete bunkers were constructed around Heysham Harbour and Home Guard trenches were dug, many of which are still visible today.

On March 13th 1941, an attempt was made to destroy the Shell Oil Refinery at Middleton where aviation fuel for Royal Air Force 'Spitfires' was being produced. A German bomber returning from an aborted night-time mission unloaded its deadly cargo in the general vicinity of the refinery. Some bombs fell in fields close to the target, while others fell on the Douglas Park housing estate demolishing a semi-detached house and killing the occupants. Another house had its front blown away but the occupants escaped injury.

When the war ended in 1945 the refinery was thought to be no longer needed and was closed down, but it was back in production by 1958 with the same two firms, Shell and ICI, jointly concerned. At first Morecambe Town Council opposed the reopening of the plant, but the protest ended when it was found that £1,000,000 in salaries and wages were going into the pay packets of workers from Morecambe and the surrounding districts.

In 1949 the son of the late Mr Walter Birtles sold the Strawberry Gardens Hotel to Messrs William Younger and Sons, the property remaining in the hands of the same company until the present day.

Miss Margaret Theodosia Twemlow Royds of Heysham Old Hall died in 1955 at the age of 90. She had come to Heysham in June 1865 as a three-month-old baby when her father, Charles Twemlow Royds, succeeded his cousin John Royds as rector of St Peter's. Apart from travelling abroad extensively in her youth, and staying frequently with friends in Cambridge, Miss

Royds lived at Heysham for the rest of her life. She lived first in the old rectory, and later (after the death of her father in March 1900) at the Old Hall with her younger

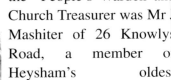

New Rectory. Completed October. 1962

RECTOR and MRS. GILLESPIE.   Photo. by courtesy of The Visitor."

From The Visitor newspaper

sister, Caroline, who died in 1924. Miss Royds, an accomplished singer, musician and composer who saw several of her works published, then lived alone in Heysham Old Hall for 31 years.

After Miss Royds' death the Old Hall was sold by Captain Charles Fletcher Twemlow (a nephew of Miss Royds) to William Mitchell Barker, Chairman of the Board of Directors of Mitchell's Brewery. The interior was remodelled and its Elizabethan character restored, and the premises opened as The Old Hall Inn in September 1958, the liquor licence having been transferred from the Wheatsheaf Hotel in Penny Street, Lancaster, which had been demolished to make room for another walk-round store.

In Heysham Village the present rectory was completed in October, 1962, after the old rectory had been demolished. The rector at the time was Albert Joseph Gillespie, and the People's Warden and Church Treasurer was Mr J Mashiter of 26 Knowlys Road, a member of Heysham's oldest surviving resident family.

In 1964 Fred Wray, as a result of ill health, old age, and the devastating effect of the continental package holiday, sold Heysham Head on behalf of the shareholders to a development company, Shearers Ltd, and the Amusement Park was demolished the following year. Only 'The Lodge' remained.

Morecambe Council, instead of buying the property outright, rented Heysham Head from Shearers Ltd in 1966 for an undisclosed figure. The deal was finalized at a secret meeting after the council chamber had been cleared of both press and public. No record of the cost of the property or the cost to the ratepayer was kept, but it has been claimed that Morecambe and Heysham ratepayers were meant to foot the bill, estimated at around £2,070,000 over a period of forty years. (Other transactions have taken place in the meantime.)

The new Heysham Head, with its main feature 'The Winged World', opened on Friday May 27th 1966. The complex eventually included a Kart Track (where it was hoped international competitions would be held), a 'Nite Club' (which appeared to be quite successful for a while), a ramshackle 'Medieval Village' (about which little can be said), and a number of bungalows intended for holiday-makers, but later taken over by the Department of Social Security (DSS).

In March 1967 a series of events were staged at Heysham to commemorate the official founding of St Peter's Church one thousand years ago as a place of Christian worship. These unique Millennium celebrations extended throughout the summer and were attended by many Christian dignitaries, including the Archbishops of York and Dublin. The events included an open-air pageant outlining the history of Heysham, a 'Festival of Flowers', an exhibition of Historic Treasures, an Art Exhibition, and a presentation in St James' Hall of the Gilbert and Sullivan opera *Iolanthe*.

Unfortunately Heysham's subsequent activities have been less prestigious. At Heysham Head, for example, none of the new attractions seemed able to compete with the old-fashioned, unsophisticated type of entertainment enjoyed by visitors in the past, and consequently 'they stayed away in their thousands'.

The saddest part of the old Heysham Head had been the sight of the tired old bear shuffling around eternally in its pit. The saddest part of the new Heysham Head was the rapidness of its decline.

Another disaster befell when British Rail, after transferring their container service from Fleetwood to Heysham at a cost of around £250,000, announced that their Sealink services were to be terminated. Heysham, at this point, appeared to be thundering along on the fast track to oblivion.

After the DSS occupation of Heysham Head site, later developments have ensured that this once widely known and well-loved recreational area has been lost forever to the general public.

In more recent time however, Heysham Village, still officially a 'protected' Conservation Area, having survived the closure of the Morecambe Bay Holiday Camp, the loss of Heysham Head, the demise of the seaside holiday, the intrusion of Nuclear Power Stations and the long and questionable interaction of planning committees and developers, appears to be arising Phoenix-like from the ashes.

Through the efforts of local organizations and individuals the still quaint and picturesque village, now floral-bedecked throughout the spring and summer, has set out to prove that there can be life after death.

Decline and Fall

Firework displays, car boot sales, rallies, open-air band concerts, festivals and romps in the rectory garden have shown that even in this age of television, computer-graphics, virtual reality and the micro-chip, simple, village-based entertainments can prove to be an attraction. Too much of an attraction at times, according to those who survived the pavement-parking, horn blaring, fume-filled nightmare of one incredibly disorganized Bank-Holiday weekend.

With rampant developers grabbing-up every square-inch of green space between Morecambe Bay and the River Lune tomorrow's people will no doubt adapt to the noise and the poisoned air and the inconsiderate behaviour, and will one day live blissfully and unconcerned in a world where no birds sing. In the meantime Heysham Village struggles bravely on with its (sometimes rained off) open-air entertainments in an attempt to recapture a little of the atmosphere of yesterday. As yet there have been no jousting knights, but you can eat, drink and be merry, and you can still find that glass of nettle beer.

--ooOoo--

Summer Event on Heysham Village Green

The History of Heysham
Index

Index